**Laura Paradis**
1430 Edgerton St
Saint Paul, MN 55130

Gary W. Hartz, PhD

# Spirituality and Mental Health
## Clinical Applications

*Pre-publication*
*REVIEWS,*
*COMMENTARIES,*
*EVALUATIONS . . .*

"Since the time of Sigmund Freud, therapists have been taught to steer clear of spiritual and religious issues in psychotherapy for fear of offending their clients, blurring professional boundaries, and reinforcing infantile wishes and fears. However, over the past several years advances in theory and research have demonstrated that the spiritual and religious beliefs of psychotherapy clients are essential features of their system for coping with problems of all kinds. In this book, Dr. Hartz teaches therapists how to unleash the power of their clients' spirituality to improve mental health and foster personal growth.

Useful to both novice and experienced therapists, this book will teach you how to assess your clients' spiritual beliefs and practices, and how to develop client-centered interventions that can channel and focus this knowledge to help them change. Dr. Hartz is a warm, thoughtful teacher who recognizes the potential problems and pitfalls in addressing spirituality and religion in clients with a wide range of beliefs and practices. He makes it clear that spirituality and religion are overlapping but distinct constructs. He asserts that spirituality is often an inseparable element in how people view the world and cope with adversity. By recognizing the potential power of these beliefs and practices, therapists can utilize them in many different interventions, targeting symptoms as diverse as depression, anxiety, posttraumatic stress, grief, identity conflicts, marital distress, chronic illness, substance abuse, and dissociation. To help therapists get started, Dr. Hartz offers examples of questions to ask clients, measures and forms that can be used to assess spirituality and religious beliefs and practices, and a complete description of how to run a time-limited psychoeducational spirituality group."

**Stephen Strack, PhD**
*Assistant Director of Training,*
*VA Ambulatory Care Center, Los Angeles;*
*Clinical Professor, Alliant International*
*University, Los Angeles, and Fuller*
*Graduate School of Psychology,*
*Pasadena, California*

*More pre-publication*
*REVIEWS, COMMENTARIES, EVALUATIONS . . .*

"*Spirituality and Mental Health* is a balanced, well-researched, and straightforward treatment of spirituality in the mental health professions that is practical and respectful of the needs of clients. Its description of the psycho-educational spirituality group is especially helpful."

**John J. Shea, PhD, MSW**
*Visiting Associate Professor*
*of Pastoral Care and Counseling,*
*Institute of Religious Education*
*and Pastoral Ministry, Boston College*

"Dr. Hartz has written a down-to-earth and practical approach to integrating the spiritual dimension into our clinical practice, regardless of our own background or beliefs. The result is a sensitive and client-centered acknowledgment of each person's need for transcendent meaning.

Dr. Hartz introduces an often neglected part of human experience that when stated becomes obvious but when neglected relegates clinical interventions to superficial status. He violates the taboo against talking with clients about their beliefs and spiritual understanding, recognizing that one's spiritual understandings, even when unreflected or unarticulated, are the core of one's coping ability. By placing spirituality under the banner of cultural competence, Dr. Hartz has honestly, simply, and pragmatically examined one of the most pervasive cultural phenomena, which profoundly affects how people cope. As a result he has spoken to the core of a large part of clinical work—namely any client for whom the meaning and purpose of life is at issue.

In our era of cultural sensitivity and competence, Dr. Hartz's book is a must-read for those who wish to recognize a personal reality that cuts across the cultures of age, place, or ethnicity—namely the particular and personal culture of spirituality with or without a belief in religion.

Dr. Hartz's exploration of spirituality provides the clinician with a systematic approach and generous references for assessing the client's understandings and beliefs from the client's point of view. He has articulated a respectful, collaborative, client-centered approach to understanding the client's meanings and coping strategies within his or her specific cultural context so as to build on a person's strengths, rather than pathologize the client's spiritual or religious experience. When a client's problems turn on religious values with which the therapist might disagree, it may seem a bit frightening, but Dr. Hartz provides guidance for the honest, respectful, and open discussion of such differences, rather than the safer road of neutrality or objectivity. I believe such an approach takes courage and sensitivity but ultimately honors the client as a valuable and whole person.

Dr. Hartz has opened the door on the difficult topic of spirituality, providing a great first step for a complicated and challenging issue."

**William L. Wallace, PhD**
*Psychologist,*
*Ocean Psychological Services,*
*Santa Monica, California*

# Spirituality
# and Mental Health
## *Clinical Applications*

# THE HAWORTH PASTORAL PRESS®
## Religion and Mental Health
### Harold G. Koenig, MD
### Senior Editor

*A Theology of God-Talk: The Language of the Heart* by J. Timothy Allen

*A Practical Guide to Hospital Ministry: Healing Ways* by Junietta B. McCall

*Pastoral Care for Post-Traumatic Stress Disorder: Healing the Shattered Soul* by Daléne Fuller Rogers

*Integrating Spirit and Psyche: Using Women's Narratives in Psychotherapy* by Mary Pat Henehan

*Chronic Pain: Biomedical and Spiritual Approaches* by Harold G. Koenig

*Spirituality in Pastoral Counseling and the Community Helping Professions* by Charles Topper

*Parish Nursing: A Handbook for the New Millennium* edited by Sybil D. Smith

*Mental Illness and Psychiatric Treatment: A Guide for Pastoral Counselors* by Gregory B. Collins and Thomas Culbertson

*The Power of Spirituality in Therapy: Integrating Spiritual and Religious Beliefs in Mental Health Practice* by Peter A. Kahle and John M. Robbins

*Bereavement Counseling: Pastoral Care for Complicated Grieving* by Junietta Baker McCall

*Biblical Stories for Psychotherapy and Counseling: A Sourcebook* by Matthew B. Schwartz and Kalman J. Kaplan

*A Christian Approach to Overcoming Disability: A Doctor's Story* by Elaine Leong Eng

*Faith, Medicine, and Science: A Festschrift in Honor of Dr. David B. Larson* edited by Jeff Levin and Harold G. Koenig

*Encyclopedia of Ageism* by Erdman Palmore, Laurence Branch, and Diana Harris

*Dealing with the Psychological and Spiritual Aspects of Menopause: Finding Hope in the Midlife* by Dana E. King, Melissa H. Hunter, and Jerri R. Harris

*Spirituality and Mental Health: Clinical Applications* by Gary W. Hartz

*Dying Declarations: Notes from a Hospice Volunteer* by David B. Resnik

*Maltreatment of Patients in Nursing Homes: There Is No Safe Place* by Diana K. Harris and Michael L. Benson

*Is There a God in Health Care? Toward a New Spirituality of Medicine* by William F. Haynes and Geffrey B. Kelly

*Guide to Ministering to Alzheimer's Patients and Their Families* by Patricia A. Otwell

# Spirituality
# and Mental Health
## *Clinical Applications*

Gary W. Hartz, PhD

The Haworth Pastoral Press®
An Imprint of The Haworth Press, Inc.
New York • London • Oxford

For more information on this book or to order, visit
http://www.haworthpress.com/store/product.asp?sku=5184

or call 1-800-HAWORTH (800-429-6784) in the United States and Canada
or (607) 722-5857 outside the United States and Canada

or contact orders@HaworthPress.com

The Haworth Pastoral Press®, an imprint of The Haworth Press, Inc., 10 Alice Street, Binghamton, NY 13904-1580.

PUBLISHER'S NOTE
Identities and circumstances of individuals discussed in this book have been changed to protect confidentiality.

The Twelve Steps are reprinted with permission of Alcoholics Anonymous World Services, Inc. (A.A.W.S.). Permission to reprint the Twelve Steps does not mean that A.A.W.S. has reviewed or approved the contents of this publication, or that A.A.W.S. necessarily agrees with the views expressed herein. A.A. is a program of recovery from alcoholism *only*—use of the Twelve Steps in connection with programs and activities which are patterned after A.A., but which address other problems, or in any other non-A.A. context, does not imply otherwise. Additionally, while A.A. is a spiritual program, A.A. is not a religious program. Thus, A.A. is not affiliated or allied with any sect, denomination, or specific religious belief.

Cover design by Marylouise E. Doyle.

**Library of Congress Cataloging-in-Publication Data**

Hartz, Gary W.
  Spirituality and mental health : clinical applications / Gary W. Hartz.
    p. cm.
  Includes bibliographical references and index.
  ISBN-13: 978-0-7890-2476-3 (hc. : alk. paper)
  ISBN-10: 0-7890-2476-4 (hc. : alk. paper)
  ISBN-13: 978-0-7890-2477-0 (pbk. : alk. paper)
  ISBN-10: 0-7890-2477-2 (pbk. : alk. paper)
  1. Mental health—Religious aspects. 2. Psychotherapy—Religious aspects. 3. Counseling—Religious aspects. 4. Spiritual life. 5. Spirituality. 6. Psychiatry and religion.
    [DNLM: 1. Religion and Psychology. 2. Counseling—methods. 3. Pastoral Care. WM 61 H338s 2005] I. Title.

RC489.R46H374 2005
616.89'14—dc22
                                                                          2004022341

This book is dedicated
to my graduate school mentor and lifelong friend,
The Reverend William L. Wallace, PhD, MDiv,
Episcopal priest and psychologist,
whose modeling, mentorship, and intellect
have helped me to grow in many ways.

# ABOUT THE AUTHOR

**Gary W. Hartz, PhD,** is a licensed psychologist at the Veterans Affairs Palo Alto Health Care System. He recently completed a part-time fellowship in ethnogeriatrics at the Stanford Geriatric Education Center, Stanford University School of Medicine. He is co-author of *Psychosocial Intervention in Long-Term Care: An Advanced Guide* (Haworth). He presents continuing education workshops on spirituality and on the mental health issues of older adults. He is a member of the American Psychological Association and Psychologists in Long-Term Care, and is an instructor at the Center for Professional Development, Santa Clara University. He currently serves as a worship coordinator at his church, where he has also conducted adult education workshops for members. He can be reached at <Gary.Hartz@med.va.gov>.

# CONTENTS

# Preface

This book has emerged only after years of personal struggle with a challenging issue: how to integrate my clients' spirituality into clinical work. Although my views about integrating spirituality are still evolving, this book provides an overview of my current approach.

In 1999 I began teaching a continuing education workshop for professionals in this area. Creating the workshop at that time was a great challenge. No one else was doing anything similar, and spirituality is such a broad area that many far-ranging topics could have been included. Consequently, in developing the workshop, I used much trial and error. Over the years I discovered what the participants valued most and least. The result is the workshop in its current form, which I have distilled into this book.

Regrettably, I cannot provide you with the experiential aspects of the workshop or with the rich discussion that we as a group enjoy. I have some ambivalence about this trade-off, because spirituality can be an exciting area to explore. For readers new to this area, providing the intellectual content without the experiential side may leave them wondering, *Why all this excitement about spirituality?* With that caveat, readers new to this field may approach this book as a theoretical frame within which they can later explore the more experiential dimensions of spirituality.

## *My Spiritual History*

It has often been said that teachers do not teach content; they teach themselves. This is especially true in an area as subjective as spirituality and mental health.

I grew up in a very devout evangelical Christian family and later attended The King's College, a fundamentalist Christian college. While studying theology at the college, I developed some doubts about my Christian faith, so I decided that I needed further study in this area. I had majored in psychology and wanted to become a psychologist, so I decided that I could meet both of these needs by attending a religiously affiliated graduate school. Consequently, I attended the Graduate School of Psychology at Fuller Theological Seminary, where I obtained a master's degree in theology and a doctorate in psychology.

While at Fuller I found myself questioning my evangelical faith more and more, until I decided that I could no longer accept either the divinity of Jesus or the inspired authority of the Bible. With these two "pillars of faith" collapsing, I retreated to an agnostic position. Naturally, this was an earth-shaking change, one that caused me anxiety and a strong sense of having lost my moorings. Fortunately, I had an advisor on the faculty, William L. Wallace, PhD, MDiv, an Episcopal priest and psychologist, who was very supportive and helped to guide me during those difficult years. I also benefited from personal psychotherapy and from my peers, some of whom were going through similar changes. During those tumultuous years of graduate school, I often attended a liberal Episcopalian church, but I still did not find it inspiring enough or compelling enough to make a commitment.

After finishing graduate school in 1982, I was left with a largely agnostic, humanistic philosophy of life. However, I always had a very strong sense that a divine being exists, however remote that being seemed at times. I did attend a Unitarian-Universalist church for a few years in the mid-1980s and was married in that church in Austin, Texas. However, soon after, we moved back to California, where I attended no church for several years. During that time I felt a very keen sense that something was missing. Fortunately, a psychiatrist at the Veterans Affairs (VA) mental health clinic where I worked was attending a Hindu Vedanta class, and invited me to attend. The classes seemed interesting, so I continued to attend them for three years. I found the ideas very helpful, particularly the notion that a unifying consciousness, or "Self," is the foundation of all life. I also found meditating on this concept to be very helpful. However, I was troubled by the teacher's constant emphasis on spiritual insight, with little emphasis on serving the larger world. Once I stopped going to these classes, I attended a Buddhist meditation group for about a year and read a great deal of Buddhist literature.

Throughout the 1990s I read most of Ram Dass's books and listened to many of his tapes. I found very compelling his synthesis of Hindu and Buddhist thought and its concrete application in the everyday world, particularly his emphasis on service. His emphasis on love and service melded very well with the similar emphasis in my Christian background.

In 1995 I again joined a Unitarian-Universalist church. My primary motive in returning to the church was to find a sense of community and a place to continue my spiritual growth.

I am currently a member of the Unitarian-Universalist Fellowship of Sunnyvale. There, I am a worship coordinator, which means that I help to plan and conduct worship services under the supervision of the minister, and that I occasionally deliver sermons. I have also taught adult education workshops related to spirituality and psychology.

So who am I now? I guess I am an eclectic, agnostic theist with Buddhist sympathies. I consider myself an agnostic in the positive, seeking sense of the word. That is, I do not think one religion has a solid handle on the sacred, and no one probably ever will. However, I think all religions have a view of the sacred that is worth examining. As such, I picture us as the "blind men and the elephant," with each person finding a valid part of the elephant but the whole eluding each one. However, going around the elephant and feeling each of the different parts is still enlightening and provocative. Instead of throwing up my hands and giving up (i.e., passive agnosticism), I see myself as a seeker on a journey of spiritual discovery.

### Overview of the Book

No book should avoid defining its terms, and few words are as ambiguous in meaning as "spirituality." I therefore begin by providing definitions of spirituality and religion in Chapter 1, along with a visual model of spirituality. The rest of the book is clinically focused. In Chapter 2 I discuss a coping model of assessment, ways to do a spiritual assessment, assessing spiritual values, and diagnostic issues. In Chapter 3 I present an ethical model for intervention based on a client-centered approach to spirituality. In Chapter 4 I provide an overview of meditation and how it can be used to enhance mental health, even when taught without religious content. In Chapter 5 I discuss the complicated issue of forgiveness, with its many controversies. In Chapter 6 I cover three specific client groups and how spirituality is particularly relevant to their issues. Finally, in Chapter 7 I describe a psychoeducational spirituality group, which can be used in mental health or church settings. A leader's guide for this group is presented in Appendix A. In Appendix B are reproducible forms that can be used as handouts for this group.

### Theme: A Client-Centered Approach

The theme woven throughout this book is that we should take a client-centered approach to integrating spirituality into our assessments and interventions. I do not use the term *client-centered* in the sense of Rogerian psychotherapy. Rather, I use it to describe our openness to clients' teaching us about what spirituality is for them; how it helps or hinders their coping; and how they can find new ways of using their spirituality to cope. In other words, we encourage clients to educate us about their spirituality, and then, if they wish, we work with them to use that spirituality to cope more effectively.

An advantage of this client-centered approach is that it is broad enough to include discussions of spirituality with agnostic and atheistic clients. Although these clients will likely describe themselves as nonreligious, they may have strong personal spiritual beliefs and practices. In this book I have tried to include assessment and intervention approaches that are broad enough to be used with such clients.

# Acknowledgments

I appreciate the helpful feedback of many colleagues and friends in formulating and refining the ideas of this book. I appreciate the reviews of Chapter 1 by two very sophisticated members of my church: Bob Lawson, JD, and Bob Clarke, PhD. I thank other members of my church for their encouraging me to publish my ideas about spirituality in a book. I appreciate the review of Chapters 4 and 5 by Janna Mitchell, MFT, who is not only a psychotherapist but also a member of my church. I thank Bruce Linenberg, PhD, for his very thorough review of and helpful suggestions for Chapter 5. I appreciate feedback from Harold Koenig, MD, on a portion of Chapter 2.

With regard to the psychoeducational spirituality group (Chapter 7 and Appendix A), I thank Chaplain Steve Haley, MDiv, of the Veterans Affairs Palo Alto Health Care System for coleading this workshop with me, so that I could include this kind of coleadership as an option in this book. This experience confirmed that a psychologist-minister team could be a useful optional partnership for facilitating the group. In developing the workshop for laypersons in a church, I thank Claire Wright, MA, MFT candidate, for coleading it with me at our church and providing valuable feedback about its content.

Finally, I wish to thank the many professionals who have attended my workshop on spirituality and mental health over the years. With their feedback I eliminated less-valuable material and included only the most pertinent concepts, applications, and insights. This book is the result of that distillation. I also thank many of them for encouraging me to translate the workshop into a book.

# Chapter 1

# Definitions of Spirituality and Religion

> In India when we meet and part we often say, "Nameste," which
> means: I honor the place in you where the entire universe re-
> sides. I honor the place in you of love, of light, of truth, of peace.
> I honor the place within you where, if you are in that place in
> you and I am in that place in me, there is only one.

> Ram Dass, 1987, *Grist for the Mill*

What is spirituality?

I have been asked this question many times. No matter how much
people read or hear about spirituality, they still seem to keep asking
this question. At my workshops on spirituality for mental health professionals, many of the participants come thirsting to know the answer to this question. What follows are my thoughts about what religion and spirituality are, including their similarities and differences.

## WHY SPIRITUALITY NOW?

Before we launch into definitions, I want to address a more basic
question: Why are so many people, mental health professionals included, so interested in spirituality now? One reason, I believe, is the
aging of the baby boomers and the ultimate questions that aging
causes them to ask. For example, how can we find meaning in life
when it all ends with death?

There are other reasons as well. In the midst of booming affluence
in the 1980s and 1990s, many people became disillusioned with traditional formulas for happiness that focus on financial gain and self-
centered pursuits. The paradox is that the wealthier we become, the
more our happiness stays the same. Myers (2000) points out that

*1*

Americans' earnings, adjusted for inflation, have more than doubled since 1957, yet our level of happiness has remained flat, and rates of depression have soared. As Gallagher (1999) puts it, "Superconsumers, we're sickened by relentless materialism. Superachievers, we're repelled by blind ambition and workaholism. 'Rugged individuals,' we feel a low-grade alienation" (p. xv). In the midst of this disillusionment and alienation, many find themselves thirsting for spiritual experience and religious community.

Other specific reasons also explain why spirituality has caught fire among mental health professionals. One is our recognition of the limits of psychotherapy and medication in helping our clients to cope, change, and flourish. Even with the best treatment, our patients often suffer intensely. Another reason is that multiculturalism is seen as an essential part of clinical work. We recognize religion and spirituality as a major part of a client's cultural world. Finally, professionals have been impressed with research studies showing that religious activity has positive associations with physical and mental health, though these associations do not prove that religion *causes* better health (see reviews by Powell, Shahabi, and Thoresen, 2003; Smith, McCullough, and Poll, 2003; and Ellison and Levin, 1998).

Why has *spirituality* rather than *religion* become the term of choice for many people? I think that many people have become dissatisfied or disillusioned with traditional religions and their institutions. Research confirms that some who identify themselves as "spiritual but not religious" have strong antireligious feelings (Spilka et al., 2003). They want to find a sacred path, but they do not want the "baggage" that comes with traditional religion. Instead, they want to create their own individual spiritual path, one that often draws eclectically from traditional religions, philosophy, popular writings on spirituality, and especially their own personal experience. Underscoring the importance of personal experience, studies show that people identifying themselves as "spiritual" are more likely to draw upon mystical and transcendent experience as a major part of their spiritual path (Spilka et al., 2003). The term *spirituality* is broad enough to describe these efforts to find connection with the sacred outside traditional religion.

However, a major problem is that the term itself is very broad and ambiguous. If you ask people to define spirituality, you will usually find them pausing and struggling. And not without reason: this is a very difficult word. What follows is my best effort to define spirituality in basic terms.

## DEFINITIONS

To define spirituality, it helps to ask first, "What is religion?" *Religion* is the search for meaning and purpose in ways related to the sacred (adapted from Pargament, 1992) or to ultimate reality (Plante and Sherman, 2001). *Sacred* means "higher powers, transcendent forces or personal beings" (Pargament, 1992, p. 205).

I believe this definition of *sacred* is broad enough to include not only the traditional God of Western religion but also such Eastern concepts of the sacred as the Tao, Brahman, or nirvana. However, some from Eastern traditions might prefer the term *ultimate reality* to *sacred*. For example, Buddhism is a nontheistic religion if one defines God as "a personal being who created the universe by deliberate design" (Smith, 1991, p. 114). On the other hand, Smith (1991) points to a second definition of God as the "Godhead," in which "the idea of personality" (p. 114) is not included. He believes that in Buddhism this second definition "stands sufficiently close to the concept of God as Godhead to warrant the name in that sense" (Smith, 1991, p. 115). To support this conclusion, he quotes the Buddha's reference to "an Unborn, neither become nor created nor formed" and points out that Buddhist texts describe nirvana as "permanent," "ageless," and "deathless" (Smith, 1991, p. 115). Nirvana, then, might be considered an ultimate reality.

Another characteristic of all religions is that they teach *morality* in one form or another. That is, they promote rules and principles promoting behavior that is "right," "just," and "good." Finally, major religions have usually given birth to *institutions* (e.g., church denominations) that form their organizational base.

Most religions would say that one of their primary goals is to develop their followers' "spirituality," but is spirituality available only to followers of religion? I think not. Religion need not be the only means for describing and connecting with the sacred or ultimate reality.

### Spirituality versus spirituality

So how do I define spirituality? I have not yet read a complete definition of spirituality that I find satisfying. Many definitions are very convoluted and vague, and dictionaries list many different dimensions in their definitions. However, to begin with, I find it useful to distinguish between *Spirituality* with a large *S* and *spirituality* with a small *s*. The difference between the two is that *Spirituality* involves the sacred or ultimate reality, whereas *spirituality* does not. However, in *Spirituality,* one's concept of the sacred or ultimate reality need not necessarily be couched in the language of religion. This is one of the most attractive features of the term *Spirituality:* the freedom to create one's own notion of the sacred or ultimate reality.

But we often use the term *spiritual* in a second sense: to describe certain psychological experiences that do not relate to the sacred or to ultimate reality. Commonly, we use it to describe powerful experiences of connecting with others or nature. For example, an elderly woman once told me that her most powerful spiritual experience was a family reunion in honor of her seventy-fifth birthday. I interpreted that to mean that she felt deeply connected to her extended family and very moved by the love they showed to her. Another woman told me that she experienced a powerful connection with nature while observing a Hawaiian volcano at close range when it was erupting at night. I do not know if these experiences included a sense of the sacred or of ultimate reality. If they did, I would label them *Spiritual* rather than *spiritual*.

Regarding *Spirituality,* it is easier to describe its primary dimensions rather than attempting a comprehensive, abstract definition. Most definitions of Spirituality include references to meaning and transcendent experience (Thoresen, 1999). To those two dimensions I would add the concept of "love." Therefore, I simply say that Spirituality has three dimensions.

1. *Meaning:* As with religion, Spirituality involves the search for meaning and purpose in ways related to the sacred or to ultimate reality. Usually, this does not involve finding an answer to the question, "What is the meaning of life?" Most often, it involves answering the question, "How does my view of the sacred or ultimate reality give my life meaning?" *Meaning* may also encom-

pass our moral principles and highest values, particularly as they emerge from our view of the sacred or ultimate reality.

2. *Transcendence:* This term refers to unitive or transpersonal experience, which gives us a sense of connecting beyond our individual selves, including a connection with the sacred or ultimate reality. I say more about transcendence later in this chapter.

3. *Love:* This reflects the moral dimension of spirituality, especially as it is motivated by beliefs related to the sacred or ultimate reality. Many spiritual teachers such as the Dalai Lama consider love to be the essence of spirituality: "Spirituality I take to be concerned with those qualities of the human spirit—such as love and compassion, patience, tolerance, forgiveness, contentment, a sense of responsibility, a sense of harmony—which bring happiness to both self and others" (The Dalai Lama, 1999, p. 22). For me, love is the place where the "rubber" of meaning and transcendence meets the "road" of life. Whether I can love reflects how seriously I take the other two dimensions of spirituality: meaning and transcendence. By *love* I do not necessarily mean an emotion. Love may simply involve an intention to do what is in the best interest of both others and myself.

I have combined these three dimensions into what I call the "primary colors" of Spirituality: meaning, transcendence, and love. These are shown as the corners of a triangle in Figure 1.1. I call these "primary colors" because although other dimensions of human experience might be called "spiritual," these can often be captured by one of the three colors or a combination of them. The three colors blend together because I see the three dimensions as constantly influencing and "dialoguing" with one another.

Admittedly, this distinction between *Spirituality* and *spirituality* is somewhat blurry. They are best viewed as the poles of a continuum, with combinations falling in between. Humanists and agnostics, for example, may fall between *Spirituality* and *spirituality.* Some humanists do not believe in the sacred and would choose human development, freedom, and dignity as their "ultimate reality" and framework of meaning. In pursuing humanistic goals, they may practice love and have transcendent experiences. They may perceive their philosophy of life as Spiritual rather than spiritual, because it involves a

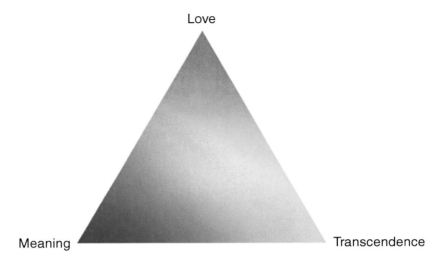

FIGURE 1.1. The Primary Colors of Spirituality (© 2005 by Gary W. Hartz.)

sense of ultimate reality and larger life purpose. Similarly, some agnostics would call themselves "spiritual but not religious." They may believe strongly in the existence of a sacred or ultimate reality yet accept not knowing or describing it. They may have powerful transcendent experiences of the sacred or ultimate reality yet remain content not to develop firm conclusions from them.

Throughout the rest of this book, I use the term *spiritual* without capitalizing it, just as I do not capitalize *religion*. However, when I use it, I will do so in the first sense previously described: that is, with a sense of the sacred or of ultimate reality involved.

## *OVERLAP BETWEEN SPIRITUALITY AND RELIGION*

All three dimensions of spirituality may be found in religion. Thus, I believe that spirituality and religion overlap, as shown in Figure 1.2. Both have in common a belief in the sacred, but each has unique traits as well. The unique traits of religion are its theology, rituals, institutions, and moral teachings. Spirituality's unique traits are its individualism and its emphasis on transcendent experience. That is, the individual may develop his or her own spiritual beliefs and practices, particularly as they are informed by personal spiritual experience.

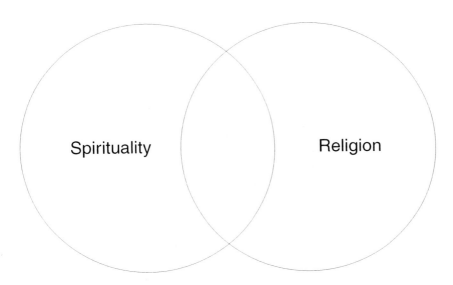

FIGURE 1.2. Overlap Between Spirituality and Religion

   Most people apparently agree that the two are distinct in some ways but overlap in others. A survey of 346 people from diverse religious backgrounds showed they believed that religion and spirituality overlap in some way: 42 percent thought that they overlap but are not the same concept, and 39 percent thought spirituality includes religion but is a broader concept (Zinnbauer et al., 1997). I agree with the former group, because I think one can practice spirituality as an individual without being affiliated with religion or its institutions.

   In real life, of course, most people do not distinguish cleanly between religion and spirituality, and many pursue a path that is a combination of the two. For example, many people who attend religious institutions cultivate a very individualistic spiritual path, in which they select their beliefs and practices not only from their own religious tradition but also from those of others. Indeed, many liberal institutions sponsor classes that help members become acquainted with the teachings and practices of various religions. Conversely, many people who consider themselves "spiritual but not religious" create their beliefs, values, and practices by drawing eclectically from religious teachings. In my experience, many of these people are particularly attracted to Buddhism because of its individual, experiential, and meditation-based methods.

## TRANSCENDENCE

Perhaps the most obscure dimension of the triangle is "transcendence." As I have mentioned, transcendence refers to unitive or transpersonal experiences that give us a sense of connecting beyond our individual selves. However, in my view, transcendent experience is only one side of the coin of transcendence. The other side might be called "perceptual transcendence," which involves a more cognitive, less experiential connection with something much larger than ourselves.

### Experiential Transcendence

Controversy abounds about what qualifies as a transcendent experience, but I have listed three types in Exhibit 1.1. Included in the exhibit are the two most common types of transcendent experiences: numinous and mystical. Although these two types can be viewed as "two poles of religious experience," they overlap and "are ultimately unified" (Spilka et al., 2003, p. 292). For example, as noted in Exhibit 1.1, mystical experiences can also be numinous when a separate, awesome "other" is experienced, be it impersonal or personal (Spilka et al., 2003). A psychological term for mystical experience is Maslow's *peak experience*, which involves "ecstatic feelings of egoless fusion with the world, of wholeness and integration, and of effortless existence in the here and now" (Wulff, 2000, p. 423).

Transcendent experiences can arise during a wide range of activities, including religious or nonreligious ones. For example, religious activities that can lead to transcendence are meditating, praying, participating in a worship service, listening to sacred music, reflecting on scriptures, or engaging in sacred dance. However, many people, religious or nonreligious, experience transcendence in contexts that are not ostensibly spiritual. These may include engaging in sex, enjoying natural beauty, having near-death experiences, relaxing deeply, or bonding intimately with a group of people. On the other hand, tran-

## EXHIBIT 1.1. Types of Transcendent Experiences

- *Sense of oneness with others*—This experience may include some feeling of connection with the sacred or ultimate       (for example, sense of union during sexual intercourse).
- *Numinous experience* (Otto, 1970)—This is a sense of awe and wonder when contemplating a Sacred Being, with the impression that the self is nothing by comparison. It occurs when we come into contact "with a mysteriousness which is both aweful and dreadful, and yet is also fascinating and compelling" (Almond, 1982, p. 54).
- *Mystical experience*—An ineffable, profound experience of "a unity which the mystic believes to be in some sense ultimate and basic to the world" (Stace, 1961, cited in Almond, 1982, p. 70). Two types of mystical experience exist:
  - —Sense of unity in which the boundaries between self and other are retained: the "other" may be impersonal or personal (Spilka et al., 2003).
  - —Oceanic oneness (cosmic consciousness): a sense of being at one with all things, animate or inanimate; a state of "absolute unitary being" in which all "boundaries of discrete being" are abolished (Newberg and d'Aquili, 1998, p. 78).

scendent experiences also can emerge when someone is doing something very mundane or experiencing something very stressful.

*Examples of Experiential Transcendence*

For readers who have not had transcendent experiences or have not heard others describe them, I provide an example here. Sophy Burnham (1997, cited in Wulff, 2000) described a mystical experience she had while visiting Machu Picchu in Peru. She was "assailed by a hollow roaring in her ears and the sense that she was there for some purpose" (Wulff, 2000, p. 398). She then describes what ensued:

> From the midst of black roaring, came a voice: *You belong to me* or *You are mine* . . . For a moment I fought it, terrified. Then: "If you are God, yes," I surrendered with my last coherent thoughts. "I belong only to God." . . . I was immersed in a sweetness words cannot express. I could hear the singing of the planets, and wave

after wave of light washed over me. But this is wrong, because I was the light as well, without distinction of self or of being washed. At one level I ceased to exist, was swallowed into light. . . . At another level, although I no longer existed as a separate "I," nonetheless I saw things, thus indicating the duality of "I" and "other." . . . I saw into the structure of the universe. I had the impression of knowing beyond knowledge and being given glimpses into ALL. (Burnham, 1997, pp. 78-79, cited in Wulff, 2000, p. 398)

Although we often think of mystical experiences as blissful, both positive and negative emotions can accompany them. In the case described, the woman was "terrified" in the beginning but as the experience went on was filled with "joy" (Wulff, 2000). Wulff (2000) describes a case in which a man whose ordinary consciousness dissolved into "a pure, absolute, abstract self" that was "without form and void of content" (James, [1902] 1985, p. 306, cited in Wulff, 2000, p. 400). As his mystical experience ended, this man "was thankful for this return from the abyss—this deliverance from so awful an initiation . . ." (James, [1902] 1985, p. 306, cited in Wulff, 2000, p. 400).

Reflecting on cases similar to these, Dittrich, von Arx, and Staub (1985) have noted that some altered states of consciousness involve the "dread of ego dissolution" (cited in Horgan, 2003, p. 13). This involves the "classic 'bad trip' in which your sense of self-dissolution is accompanied not by bliss but by negative emotions, from mild uneasiness to full-blown terror and paranoia" (Horgan, 2003, p. 13). Religious mystics have also noted these potential negative experiences. For example, in Christian mysticism there is the "dark night of the soul," in which joyous illumination "fades away and a state of emptiness, misery, and chaos takes its place" (Wulff, 2000, p. 415). When people find these experiences highly disturbing, they have sometimes been called "spiritual emergencies" (Wulff, 2000).

### Perceptual Transcendence

Many people have not had transcendent experiences and may be incapable of having them, yet they long to have these powerful encounters. Can these people access transcendence in any way? I think they can through *perceptual transcendence*. Perceptual transcendence involves a shift in our perspective so that we can see the "big picture" provided by our spiritual philosophy. Perceptual transcendence may or may not be accompanied by *transcendent experience*. As such, the person may experience more of a cognitive shift than an experiential unity. For example, when some religious followers find their problems overwhelming, they are comforted by their conviction that, despite all these difficulties, "God has a plan" or "God is in charge." Other religious people might choose to see the world, others, and themselves "as God sees them," placing everything in cosmic perspective. An analogy would be looking at planet Earth from the space shuttle: suddenly our "huge world" with all of its "big problems" takes on an emotional distance. We can see that we are part of a much larger universe.

### Additional Resources

From an academic and philosophical standpoint, my discussion of transcendence has touched only the surface. For in-depth reviews of theoretical and empirical literature on mystical experience and altered states of consciousness, please see books by Spilka and colleagues (2003) and Cardena, Lynn, and Krippner (2000).

## CONCLUSION

The controversy over differentiating spirituality and religion may never be resolved. However, in this chapter I have given you my best effort at outlining their similarities and differences. The remainder of this book will be clinically focused, starting with assessment of spirituality as it interfaces with mental health issues.

# Chapter 2

# Assessment of Spirituality

Unfortunately, many clinicians miss very important information about their clients because they have never asked. One of these areas is often spirituality. Beginning with the first session, clinicians who do not ask about spirituality in their assessments can miss an opportunity to build rapport with religious clients and to account for their clients' perspective during interventions. If we do not ask, we may not know, because many clients hesitate to initiate the topic.

My approach throughout this book is to take a client-centered approach to assessing spirituality and integrating it into treatment. The purpose of this chapter is to provide a client-centered road map for briefly assessing a client's spirituality. I first provide a basic theoretical framework for assessing spirituality, one that is rooted in Pargament's (1997) coping theory. I then discuss interview questions and a written instrument for assessing spirituality. For clients whose lives are in a period of transition or rapid change, I provide a values clarification instrument that includes spiritually related values. With regard to diagnostic issues, I discuss DSM-IV-TR's diagnosis of "religious or spiritual problem." Finally, I address three issues related to differentiating religious experience from psychiatric disorder.

## A COPING MODEL OF ASSESSMENT

Before discussing specific techniques for assessing spirituality, I first describe a model for understanding the interaction between spirituality and mental health. The model is that described by Ken Pargament, a leading researcher and theoretician in the field of the psychology of religion. In his book *The Psychology of Religion and Coping* (Pargament, 1997), he presents a very detailed description of his complex theory. I describe here what I consider to be his core ideas that are most relevant to clinical practice.

The main idea is that we all have a basic framework for understanding life, spoken or unspoken, that colors how we react to stressful events. Pargament (1997) calls this basic interpretive framework an "orienting system," which is a "general way of viewing and dealing with the world" (p. 99). Specifically, it consists of our "habits, values, relationships, generalized beliefs, and personality" (Pargament, 1997, p. 100). Practically, it is a "frame of reference, a blueprint of oneself and the world that is used to anticipate and come to terms with life's events" (Pargament, 1997, p. 100). We use this orienting system during difficult times and may find it to be "a help or a hindrance in the coping process" (Pargament, 1997, p. 100). The orienting system, then, is an interpretive lens through which someone perceives the events of life, be they negative or positive. This lens may be religious or nonreligious in content.

This orienting system not only serves as an interpretive framework but also influences how we choose to cope with stress. These ways of coping consist of the "concrete thoughts, feelings, behaviors, and interactions" that we use during difficult times (Pargament, 1997, p. 104). Pargament (1997) contends that in coping with stress, we do one of two things with our orienting system: (1) we "conserve" our basic orienting system, using it to cope and continuing to believe in it; or (2) we "transform" it in some way, because we do not find it useful in coping, or find ourselves questioning it in the face of the stressor. No rule determines whether conserving or transforming our views is more helpful: either one can be helpful or harmful, depending on the person and the stressors faced (Pargament, 1997).

To offer an extreme example, Pargament (1997) describes a young woman who had just suffered a car accident "that killed members of her family, almost killed her, and left her with chronic, incapacitating pain" (p. 110). Prior to the accident, she had been "energetic, popular, and optimistic, looking forward to college, marriage, and a productive life" (Pargament, 1997, p. 110). After the accident, she lost "many of the things she cared about most deeply—friends, family, jobs, vitality, and independence" (p. 110). In other words, she had lost the basic orienting system that had served her well up to this point in life. In this case trying to conserve it would have been hopeless; she had to transform her orienting system in some way to cope with current realities. On the other hand, if her orienting system had included a religious perspective and practices, that part of her orienting system could have been preserved in some way. For example, her religious beliefs might have provided her with a basis for understanding why devout followers might experience such devastating losses, as well as what role a deity plays in such. They might also have provided her with concrete ways of coping, such as prayer or religious rituals.

## The Coping Model in Clinical Terms

To make this model more concrete, I now describe it in more clinical terms. To begin, we must view religious coping in the context of other, nonreligious methods of coping. As we face stressful events, various "stress buffers" help us cope. These include our social support network, biological resilience, and general coping skills. Another potential stress buffer is our appraisal of the stressor as threatening or not, and our ability to cope with it (Pargament, 1997). The more we perceive the stressor as threatening and the less we believe we can cope with it, the higher our stress load. A stress buffer of central interest to us is one that I call "sources of meaning," and which Pargament (1997) calls our orienting system. These sources of meaning can include religion and spirituality, family, career, community, and material possessions, among others. They form the cornerstones of our lives, giving us meaning and purpose. Often, these are such implicit parts of our lives that we may scarcely notice how much they contribute to buffering our stress.

These stress buffers are not exclusive and may interact with one another. The interrelationship among the buffers is shown in Figure 2.1. Although spirituality and religion are not listed in this figure, they are assumed to be one piece of the Sources of Meaning sphere. That area, in turn, is related to all of the other stress buffers.

To take a simple example of how spirituality and religion relates to the other buffers, suppose a woman's husband has been hospitalized with a sudden, life-threatening illness. Her religion might help her to cope in the following interrelated ways. First, her belief that "God will help us through it" may decrease her perception of the stressor as threatening and enhance her confidence in her ability to cope. Her religion may provide her with coping skills, such as prayer or scriptural reading. Her minister and fellow congregants may provide her with

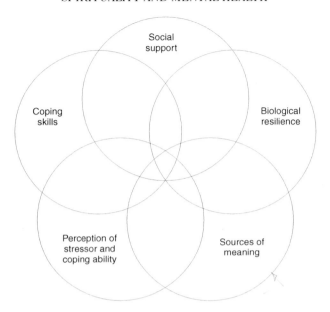

FIGURE 2.1. Interrelationship of Stress Buffers

social support. All of those buffers may, in turn, help to enhance her biological resilience by bolstering her immune system and reducing the physical stress she experiences from negative emotions. Of course, in this example, I have presented a woman who experiences positive benefits from her religion in coping with this stressor. Another religious person could experience negative effects from religious coping, which also could negatively impact the other buffers.

Of the five stress buffers, we are most interested in Sources of Meaning because it includes religion and spirituality. Most of us have other sources of meaning as well, some of which are more important than others. As such, each of us has a hierarchy of sources of meaning, which I have shown as a pyramid in Figure 2.2. Some sources of meaning are foundational, others secondary, and others marginal. For example, for one person *family* might provide a foundational framework of meaning, *religion* a secondary one, and *career* a more marginal one.

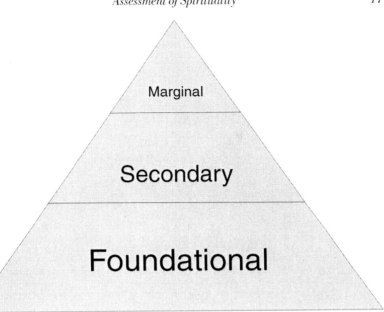

FIGURE 2.2. Hierarchy of Sources of Meaning

## APPLICATION OF THE MODEL
## TO CLINICAL PRACTICE

In clinical practice it is very important that we discover whether clients' sources of meaning include religion and how important that is to them. If clients value religion very strongly, then we should take time to include a spiritual assessment as part of our initial evaluation. If they have no religion or it is not highly valued, then the clinician could skip such an assessment.

Those who have religion or spirituality as a primary source of meaning might not volunteer such information unless asked. One way to do this is to ask a simple screening question on an intake form or during the intake interview. One possible question is, "Do you have spiritual beliefs or practices that help you cope with your problems?"

If clients answer negatively or describe only a minimal religious orientation, then we need not ask more. If they indicate that spirituality is an important source of strength for them, then you can ask basic questions about their religious affiliation, belief in a higher being, and religious practices. Once they have described these, you can ask questions about how they practice their spirituality and how it helps them to cope. Examples of some of these questions are listed in Exhibit 2.1. Most of these questions involve the "what" and "how" of

---

**EXHIBIT 2.1. Interview Questions
for Assessing a Person's Use of Religion in Coping**

*For all persons:*

- Membership: religious affiliation, denominational membership.
- Belief in God or higher being.
- Religious practices: prayer, meditation, other rituals.

*For religious persons:*

- What purpose does religion serve in your life?
- How is religion involved in the way you cope with your present problems?

*For members of religious organizations:*

- How did you become affiliated with your denomination?
- What congregational activities are most important to you and why?
- How have your minister and fellow members been involved in helping you with your current problems?

*For those who pray or meditate:*

- What do you pray for? Do you use prayer to help with your current problems?
- How do you meditate? Do you use meditation to help with your current problems?

*For those who believe in God:*

- How do you envision God? What type of relationship do you have with God? How has this changed over the years?
- How has this relationship affected the way you are dealing with your current problems?

*Source:* Adapted from Pargament, 1997, p. 374.

religious belief and practice. For example, those who pray can be asked what they pray for and how it helps them to cope.

Another way of following up the screening item is to give clients a brief questionnaire, such as the Religious Background and Behaviors Questionnaire (CASAA, 1994), which is presented in Exhibit 2.2. Notice that the first question concerns spiritual orientation. The re-

## EXHIBIT 2.2. The Religious Background and Behaviors Questionnaire

1. Which of the following best describes you at the present time? (Check one.)

_____ Atheist: I do not believe in a sacred being or supreme reality, such as God, Brahman, Allah, or nirvana.

_____ Agnostic: I believe we can't really know about a sacred being or supreme reality, such as God, Brahman, Allah, or nirvana.

_____ Unsure: I don't know what to believe about a sacred being or supreme reality, such as God, Brahman, Allah, or nirvana.

_____ Spiritual: I'm not religious, but I believe in a sacred being or supreme reality, such as God, Brahman, Allah, or nirvana.

_____ Religious: I practice religion and believe in a sacred being or supreme reality, such as God, Brahman, Allah, or nirvana.

2. For the *past year,* how often have you done the following? (Circle one number for each line.)

| | Never | Rarely | Once or twice a month | Once or twice a week | Almost daily | More than once a day |
|---|---|---|---|---|---|---|
| a. Thought about a sacred being or supreme reality | 1 | 2 | 3 | 4 | 5 | 6 |
| b. Prayed | 1 | 2 | 3 | 4 | 5 | 6 |
| c. Meditated | 1 | 2 | 3 | 4 | 5 | 6 |

*(continued)*

*(continued)*

| | | | | | | |
|---|---|---|---|---|---|---|
| d. Attended religious services | 1 | 2 | 3 | 4 | 5 | 6 |
| e. Read scriptures or holy writings | 1 | 2 | 3 | 4 | 5 | 6 |
| f. Had direct experiences of a sacred being or supreme reality | 1 | 2 | 3 | 4 | 5 | 6 |

3. Have you *ever* in your life:

| | Never | Yes, in the past but not now | Yes, and I still do |
|---|---|---|---|
| a. Believed in a sacred being or supreme reality? | 1 | 2 | 3 |
| b. Prayed? | 1 | 2 | 3 |
| c. Meditated? | 1 | 2 | 3 |
| d. Attended religious services regularly? | 1 | 2 | 3 |
| e. Read or studied scriptures or holy writings regularly? | 1 | 2 | 3 |
| f. Had direct experiences of a sacred being or supreme reality? | 1 | 2 | 3 |

*Source:* Adapted from Center on Alcoholism, Substance Abuse and Addictions, 1994.

maining questions concern six religious activities, asking how frequently the clients do them now and whether they did them in the past. For the questions about present practices, the clinician can follow up with the "what" and "how" questions. For the questions about lifelong practices, the clinician can note where clients had indicated "Yes, in the past but not now." These items provide an opportunity to understand clients' spiritual histories.

Some clinicians doing longer-term psychotherapy like to take an in-depth spiritual history with clients for whom religion is a central source of meaning. A spiritual history can involve questions about clients' experiences with religion during childhood, adolescence, and adulthood; their most positive and negative experiences with religion;

how spirituality has helped or hindered their efforts to cope with life crises; and, if clients believe in a higher being, how their way of relating to that being has changed over time. Taking a detailed history would appear especially important when clients have experienced some serious changes in religious orientation or practices over their lifetimes. Another benefit is that it can alert the clinician to wounding experiences that they have encountered in religious contexts.

## Assessing Religion in the Context of Other Coping Methods

I pause here to underscore the importance of context in assessing religious coping. Occasionally religious clients talk in purely religious terms about a problem or their way of coping with it, as if the only perspective or coping method is religious. In fact, for most of these clients religion is *not* the only way that they cope. Obviously, clinicians must explore the client's entire range of coping methods, not just religious ones. As Pargament (1997) states,

> Religious coping has to be assessed in the context of nonreligious coping methods and goals. For example, the client who describes an illness as God's will is not necessarily discounting the role of other important causal factors. God may be seen as acting in concert with other personal, social, and biological forces or apart from them. Only by exploring religious and nonreligious patterns of attribution can it be determined whether the individual is making an error of explanation. . . . In short, the assessment of religion from a coping perspective requires a judicious weighing and balancing of a dynamic array of situational, social and personal forces. (p. 376)

Once the clinician has a sense of the client's "dynamic array" of resources for coping, including religious ones, he or she is in a powerful position to integrate them meaningfully into treatment.

## Case Example

A middle-aged man presented for treatment with anxiety and depression. One cause of his depression was his progressive, very painful back problem, which prevented him from working and doing usual recreational activities. This back problem caused him a great deal of anxiety because he wondered how quickly he would become even more disabled. I asked him my usual screening question, "Do you have spiritual beliefs or practices that help you cope with these problems?" He replied that he definitely did. He said that he had been a practicing Catholic for many years but left that religion ten years ago and began studying Native American religions. During the past five years he had adopted eclectic Native American religious beliefs and practices. Because of his strong faith, I administered the Religious Background and Behaviors Questionnaire. On this scale he endorsed the items and explained his responses in the following ways:

- *Items "a" and "b":* He "thought about God" and "prayed" more than once a day. Asked to whom he prayed, he said he prayed to the "ancestors, Creator, and 4 Winds." Asked what he prayed for, he prayed "for guidance" from the Creator and ancestors. Concerning how prayer helped, he said that praying strengthened his "faith and hope" that the future would be better.
- *Item "c":* Concerning "meditation," he did so "almost daily." Asked about whether his anxiety and pain distracted him during meditation, he said that he was able to stay present-focused during meditation. Consequently, during meditation he experienced a reduction in his anxiety.
- *Item "d":* He reported that he rarely "attended worship services" of the Native American tradition.
- *Item "e":* Concerning reading or studying "scriptures" or "holy writings," he studied Native American scriptures almost daily. He found that it reduced his anxiety by focusing his mind elsewhere.
- *Item "f":* Concerning "direct experiences of God," he said that he had these almost daily. Asked what kind of experiences these were, he described experiences of "connecting with a Higher Being"; "being guided to places by a Higher Being"; and "communicating with Ancestors in dreams."

*Comment:* Notice that, in interviewing him about his responses on the questionnaire, I discovered more than simply what his religious practices were. In asking him about the impact of these practices on his presenting problems, I discovered that these helped to reduce his anxiety and to provide him with hope.

## POSITIVE AND NEGATIVE RELIGIOUS COPING

What are the kinds of religious coping for which the clinician can listen? Pargament (1997) emphasizes that religious coping can be either positive or negative in its effect on coping. That is, it may help or hinder a person's efforts to cope. Pargament (1997) describes common positive means of religious coping, some of which are listed in

Table 2.1. A theme among these is that religion is seen as a means of great support: God, religious leaders, and fellow congregants are all seen as allies in overcoming difficulties. Empirical studies have found that these types of religious coping mechanisms are associated with better outcomes in physical and mental health when people deal with life stress (Pargament, 1997). When a client describes these positive means of coping, the clinician can ask the client to describe which problems the methods help with and how.

On the other side of the coin, Pargament (1997; Pargament et al.,1998) has described negative means of religious coping, which he calls "religious red flags," some of which are listed in Table 2.2. Here, the theme is just the opposite of that in the positive means of coping: the person feels alienated or in conflict with God, religious leaders, or fellow congregants. Empirical studies have found that

TABLE 2.1. Empirically Supported Methods of Religious Coping Associated with Better Mental/Physical Adjustment to Stressful Events

| Religious Coping Method | Description |
|---|---|
| Spiritual support and collaborative coping | Belief that one is receiving support and guidance from God; God seen as another member of one's support network<br><br>Examples follow:<br>• Help in problem solving: "God is showing me how to deal with this."<br>• Emotional reassurance: "I trust God would not let anything terrible happen to me."<br>• Nurturing a close spiritual relationship: "I seek God's love and care." |
| Congregational support | Helpfulness of clergy, lay leaders, and fellow congregants in times of stress |
| Benevolent religious reframing | Attributing the stressful event to the will of God or to a loving God<br><br>Examples follow:<br>• God's control: "God is in control of the outcome of my illness."<br>• God seen as just, loving, and benevolent: "I trust that God is doing what is best for me." |

*Source:* Adapted from Pargament, 1997.

TABLE 2.2. Red Flags in Religious Coping

| Religious Perception/Feeling | Description |
| --- | --- |
| Discontentment with God | Perception that one has been abandoned or disappointed by God, often accompanied by anger and resentment |
| Perception of God's punishment | Perception that God has caused the stressful event as punishment |
| Discontentment with congregation | Perception that one's religious leaders or fellow congregants have failed to provide support, or have given advice/teachings with which one disagrees |
| Religious doubt or apathy | Questioning or giving up previously held religious beliefs about God, others, and self |

*Source:* Adapted from Pargament, 1997, and Pargament et al., 1998.

these types of negative religious coping mechanisms are associated with worse outcomes in mental and physical health when people deal with life stress (Pargament, 1997). When a client describes these negative means of coping, Pargament and colleagues (1998) recommend exploring these carefully to see whether they are contributing to a client's distress and difficulty coping. However, Pargament (1997) also cautions that we cannot presume that their effects are always negative for everyone. He states, "The red flags were not designed to be definitive indicators of problems; rather they were meant to alert the counselor to statements that signal the need for further religious exploration" (Pargament, 1997, p. 375). For example, for some people anger at God may be a temporary reaction to stress that, over the long run, triggers a deeper spiritual search or a revised view of God.

One caution here is that the studies identifying these positive and negative means of coping are cross-sectional in nature. That is, after a stressful event occurred, the researchers measured how people adapted and whether certain coping methods were associated with better or worse outcomes in mental and physical health. This type of study does not establish that the methods of coping *caused* the better or worse outcome, only that an association was present. The suggestive nature of these studies, then, underscores the importance of taking a client-centered approach to assessing the impact of coping methods on any given client. As Pargament and colleagues (1998) state, "Some expressions of religion may be red flags warning of trouble, others may be yellow flags calling for caution and further assessment, still others may be green flags indicating that religion is facilitating the process of coping" (p. 88).

## Religious Red Flags: Clinical Examples

### Case 1

A thirty-year-old married mother presented with depression caused by several years of severe migraine headaches and separate periods of nausea and vomiting. These were adversely affecting her marriage, because they restricted her ability to travel and limited how much time she could spend with her three-year-old daughter. She had been referred for evaluation of a possible psychosomatic disorder, because no clear medical causes and no successful treatment had been found.

She was an evangelical Christian and an active member of her church. She found that Bible reading and Christian music helped relieve her depression.

On the Beck Depression Inventory she circled following the item: "I feel I am being punished." Asked how and why, she said, "I can't understand why God would make me sick." Asked what she meant, she said that since her prayers for a cure had gone unanswered, God must have been "making" her sick to punish her for something.

*Comment:* I saw her only for evaluation but had I seen her for therapy, I would have wanted to explore her theological reasons for believing this. I would also have explored the possibility of obtaining a release to contact her minister. If I had contacted the minister, I would have asked him about her belief that God must be punishing her because she had not been healed. If he offered other, less judgmental explanations, I would have suggested that she and he meet to discuss the issue.

### Case 2

A middle-aged, former Pentecostal minister was admitted to a residential psychiatric unit with severe depression because of a recent stroke, divorce, and subsequent alienation from his children. To assess his depression, I administered the Beck Depression Inventory. Here he checked the item, "I feel I am being punished." Asked about this, he explained that, in the aftermath of his divorce, he had lived with his elderly mother for a while. During that time, his judgment and impulse control were poor, which she found very distressing. After several months of living with her, she suffered a stroke, which he attributed to all the stress he had created for her. He believed that God was now punishing him with the divorce and subsequent painful alienation from his family. He requested to talk with a Pentecostal minister about this issue. I then spoke to the VA chaplain, who talked with him about this. Unfortunately, the patient's cognitive impairment did not permit them to have a meaningful examination of the issues. However, as time went on, the patient did not appear preoccupied with this issue of punishment, and his mood improved quickly.

## ASSESSING VALUES: "WHERE AM I GOING?"

Often the clients we see are coping with a life crisis of some kind. As a result, they come to us in transition, questioning old directions and values and seeking new ones. Those recovering from substance abuse, for example, often describe a dramatic change in their values: from self-centered ones to those affirming relationships, spirituality, and community. I will have more to say about life transitions in Chapter 6, in the section titled Clients in Crisis: Crisis As Danger and Opportunity.

### Values Clarification Instrument

Although clients often describe their changing values for us, it is sometimes useful to have them prioritize their emerging values using a values clarification instrument. I like to use a contemporary list of values derived from the Personal Values Card Sort developed by Miller and colleagues (2001). This card sort consists of eighy-three values that clients can prioritize for themselves. I have collated these values into a values survey, shown in Exhibit 2.3, which clients use to rate their five top values. No norms are available, and thus this is not a scored instrument.

Once clients have rated their values, you "can review their rankings with them and encourage them to explain and elaborate on why they ranked the values the way they did" (Richards, Rector, and Tjeltveit, 1999, p. 153). You can also ask them "to explore how these values are expressed or manifested in their lives and to examine whether their behavior and lifestyle choices are consistent with their professed values" (Richards, Rector, and Tjeltveit, 1999, p. 153).

Many options are available for administering this values survey. For example, clinicians may wish to have clients rate their top ten values rather than their top five. They can also have clients rate their bottom five or ten.

## EXHIBIT 2.3. Values Survey

The purpose of this exercise is to help you identify what you value most, so that you can set meaningful life goals and treatment goals.

Following is a list of eighty-three values. Please read through the list and identify the five values that are most important to you. Do this in two steps. First, as you read the values, place a check mark beside those that are very important to you. Then, looking over those checked, designate your top five values by numbering them 1 to 5, with 1 being the most important.

### *List of Values*

_____ Acceptance: to be accepted as I am

_____ Accuracy: to be correct in my opinions and actions

_____ Achievement: to accomplish and achieve

_____ Adventure: to have new and exciting experiences

_____ Attractiveness: to be physically attractive

_____ Authority: to be in charge of others

_____ Autonomy: to be self-determining and independent

_____ Beauty: to appreciate beauty around me

_____ Caring: to take care of others

_____ Challenge: to take on difficult tasks and problems

_____ Change: to have a life full of change and variety

_____ Comfort: to have a pleasant, enjoyable life

_____ Commitment: to make a long-lasting and deep commitment to another person

_____ Compassion: to feel and show concern for others

_____ Contribution: to make a contribution that will last after I am gone

_____ Cooperation: to work collaboratively with others

_____ Courtesy: to be polite and considerate to others

*(continued)*

*(continued)*

_____ Creativity: to have new and original ideas

_____ Dependability: to be reliable and trustworthy

_____ Duty: to carry out my duties and responsibilities

_____ Ecology: to live in harmony with and protect the environment

_____ Excitement: to have a life full of thrills and stimulation

_____ Faithfulness: to be loyal and reliable in relationships

_____ Fame: to be known and recognized

_____ Family: to have a loving, happy family

_____ Fitness: to be physically fit and strong

_____ Flexibility: to adjust to new or unusual situations easily

_____ Forgiveness: to be forgiving of others

_____ Friendship: to have close, supportive friends

_____ Fun: to play and have fun

_____ Generosity: to give what I have to others

_____ Genuineness: to behave in a manner that is true to who I am

_____ God's will: to seek and obey the will of God

_____ Growth: to keep changing and growing

_____ Health: to be physically well and healthy

_____ Helpfulness: to be helpful to others

_____ Honesty: to be truthful and genuine

_____ Hope: to maintain a positive and optimistic outlook

_____ Humility: to be modest and unassuming

_____ Humor: to see the humorous side of myself and the world

_____ Independence: to be free from depending on others

_____ Industry: to work hard and well at my life tasks

_____ Inner peace: to experience personal peace

_____ Intimacy: to share my innermost experience with others

_____ Justice: to promote equal and fair treatment for all

_____ Knowledge: to learn and possess valuable knowledge

_____ Leisure: to take time to relax and enjoy

_____ Loved: to be loved by those close to me

_____ Loving: to give love to others

_____ Mastery: to be competent in my everyday activities

_____ Mindfulness: to live conscious and mindful of the present moment

_____ Moderation: to avoid excesses and find a middle ground

_____ Monogamy: to have one close, loving relationship

_____ Nonconformity: to question and challenge authority and norms

_____ Nurturance: to take care of and nurture others

_____ Openness: to be open to new experiences, ideas, and options

_____ Order: to have a life that is well-ordered and organized

_____ Passion: to have deep feelings about ideas, activities, or people

_____ Pleasure: to feel good

_____ Popularity: to be well-liked by many people

_____ Power: to have control over others

_____ Purpose: to have meaning and direction in my life

_____ Rationality: to be guided by reason and logic

_____ Realism: to see and act realistically and practically

_____ Responsibility: to make and carry out important decisions

_____ Risk: to take risks and chances

*(continued)*

*(continued)*

_____ Romance: to have intense, exciting love in my life

_____ Safety: to be safe and secure

_____ Self-acceptance: to like myself as I am

_____ Self-control: to be self-disciplined and govern my own actions

_____ Self-esteem: to feel positive about myself

_____ Self-knowledge: to have a deep, honest understanding of myself

_____ Service: to be of service to others

_____ Sexuality: to have an active and satisfying sex life

_____ Simplicity: to live life simply, with minimal needs

_____ Solitude: to have time and space where I can be apart from others

_____ Spirituality: to grow and mature spiritually

_____ Stability: to have a life that stays fairly consistent

_____ Tolerance: to accept and respect those different from me

_____ Tradition: to follow respected patterns of the past

_____ Virtue: to live a morally pure and excellent life

_____ Wealth: to have plenty of money

_____ World peace: to work to promote peace in the world

*Source:* Adapted from Miller et al., 2001.

In responding to this questionnaire, some clients have mentioned difficulties in rating the values. One challenge is that many of the words are synonyms, so clients may have trouble deciding among similar terms. However, for clients who are particular about precise meanings, there are lots of choices. Another issue is the primary sphere of life in which the client looks at these values. For example, in rating these values, is the client thinking primarily of work life, family life, leisure life, spiritual life, a combination, or no context in particular? Clients who express this concern could assign different ratings for separate areas of life or simply decide, as most do, to take multiple contexts into account when doing the ratings. A final issue relates to which "self" the client is rating: is it the "real self" of today or the "ideal self" that one is striving to become? The clinician should ask, as suggested previously, about the extent to which the client believes he or she is living out these values.

## THE DSM-IV'S DIAGNOSIS
## OF RELIGIOUS OR SPIRITUAL PROBLEM

Concerning diagnostic issues, the *Diagnostic and Statistical Manual of Mental Disorders,* Fourth Edition Text Revised (American Psychiatric Association, 2000) lists a diagnosis of "Religious or Spiritual Problem." This diagnosis is used "when the focus of clinical attention is a religious or spiritual problem" (American Psychiatric Association, 2000, p. 741. Reprinted with permission from the *Diagnostic and Statistical Manual of Mental Disorders,* Text Revision, Copyright 2000. American Psychiatric Association). Examples include "distressing experiences that involve loss or questioning of faith, problems associated with conversion to a new faith, or questioning of spiritual values that may not necessarily be related to an organized church or religious institution" (American Psychiatric Association, 2000, p. 741. Reprinted with permission from the *Diagnostic and Statistical Manual of Mental Disorders,* Text Revision, Copyright 2000. American Psychiatric Association). The diagnosis might also be used for other religious problems. For example, it could be used for a client struggling with questions arising from near-death or mystical experiences.

This diagnosis is a V Code in the DSM-IV-TR section titled Other Conditions That May Be a Focus of Clinical Attention. It is coded on Axis I and may stand by itself or be related to other Axis I and II diagnoses.

## RELIGIOUS ISSUES AND PSYCHIATRIC DISORDERS

Although religion can directly influence many psychiatric symptoms, three diagnostic areas are particularly affected: obsessive-compulsive disorder (OCD), psychotic disorders, and dissociative disorders. How religious beliefs and practices can affect each of these disorders is discussed next. I also offer some guidelines for differentiating psychopathology from intense but psychologically "normal" experiences associated with clients' religious culture.

### *Obsessive-Compulsive Disorder*

In religious clients obsessive-compulsive disorder may be expressed in part by excessive perfectionism, obsessive self-scrutinization, and compulsive performing of rituals. Mora (1969, cited in Spilka et al., 2003) has termed this *scrupulosity,* which is considered a religious subtype of OCD. Scrupulosity involves obsessively worrying about spiritual issues or feeling compelled to complete certain religious rituals (Askin et al., 1993, cited in Spilka et al., 2003). Askin and colleagues (1993) developed a measure of scrupulosity which, as expected, was highly correlated with symptoms of OCD.

Clients with scrupulosity may present with obsessions such as fear of sinning and compulsive doubt, which may lead them to seek repeated reassurance from religious authority figures (Spilka et al., 2003). On the compulsive side, they may engage in rigid ritualistic practices in order to gain absolute acceptance and forgiveness from God (Spilka et al., 2003). Often, they never see themselves as acceptable to God because they insist on viewing themselves as sinful and the deity as "unforgiving and tolerating no deviation from extreme religious strictures" (Spilka et al., 2003, p. 511).

The clinician must explore the nature of the client's religious teachings, institution, and congregation. Some highly controlling and demanding religious groups promote this kind of obsessive religiosity. Thus, it is essential to sort out how much the client's religious OCD is a reflection of his or her religious subculture, versus a product of his own personal processes.

## Dissociative Disorders versus Religiously Oriented Dissociative States

It is very important to distinguish between dissociative disorders and dissociative states. According to the DSM-IV-TR (American Psychiatric Association, 2000), dissociative disorders involve "a disruption in the usually integrated functions of consciousness, memory, identity, or perception of the environment," which causes distress or interferes with occupational and social functioning (p. 519. Reprinted with permission from the *Diagnostic and Statistical Manual of Mental Disorders,* Text Revision, Copyright 2000. American Psychiatric Association.). On the other hand, dissociative *states,* which can also involve disturbances of consciousness and perception, are a "common and accepted expression of cultural activities or religious experience in many societies" (American Psychiatric Association, 2000, p. 519. Reprinted with permission from the *Diagnostic and Statistical Manual of Mental Disorders,* Text Revision, Copyright 2000. American Psychiatric Association). The DSM-IV emphasizes that a dissociative state by itself "should not be considered inherently pathological and often does not lead to significant distress, impairment, or help-seeking behavior" (American Psychiatric Association, 2000, p. 519. Reprinted with permission from the *Diagnostic and Statistical Manual of Mental Disorders,* Text Revision, Copyright 2000. American Psychiatric Association.). For example, hypnosis can be a dissociative state that is used psychotherapeutically. Similarly, many religious groups encourage their followers to enter into dissociative states, which might also be called "altered states of awareness." Religious people may experience dissociative states during rituals such as speaking in tongues, healing, religious dancing, or communicating with spirits or a divine being.

When does a religiously oriented dissociative state become a dissociative disorder? A helpful guideline is suggested by the DSM-IV-TR's criteria for dissociative trance disorder, a diagnosis for further study in the DSM-IV-TR. This diagnosis is made only if (1) the observed "trance state is not accepted as a normal part of a collective cultural or religious practice" and (2) the trance causes "clinically significant distress" or social and occupational impairment (American Psychiatric Association, 2000, p. 785. Reprinted with permission from the *Diagnostic and Statistical Manual of Mental Disorders,*

Text Revision, Copyright 2000. American Psychiatric Association.).
Thus, to diagnose the trance state as psychopathological, the clinician
must have thorough knowledge of the religious tradition in which the
client participates. Otherwise, the clinician cannot determine whether
it deviates from the norms of that religious subculture. Obviously,
this may call for the clinician's educating himself or herself about that
religious tradition or consulting with others who do know it.

On the other hand, this is only a guideline, not a rule. Even when
people engage in dissociative rituals that are consistent with their religious tradition, some may have psychopathological reactions or use
them in extreme, compulsive ways that interfere with social and occupational functioning.

### Psychotic Experiences with Religious Content

When religious clients describe hallucinations with religious content, clinicians are naturally concerned about the possibility of psychosis. Some religious people describe experiences of talking with
and seeing religious figures, such as the Virgin Mary or Jesus. The
Catholic Church has recognized "apparitions of the Virgin Mary
throughout history," and "visions of Jesus Christ occur within both
Catholicism and Protestantism" (Spilka et al., 2003, pp. 272, 276).
For example, St. Teresa of Avila reported that the Virgin Mary appeared to her and clothed her "in a robe of great whiteness and clar-
ity," which purified her of sin and gave her "the greatest joy and bliss"
(Warner, 1976, p. 301). St. Teresa describes what happened next:

> Our Lady seemed suddenly to seize me by the hands. She told
> me that I was giving her great pleasure by serving the glorious
> St. Joseph, and promised me that my plans for the convent
> would be fulfilled . . . then she seemed to hang around my neck a
> very beautiful gold collar from which hung a cross of great
> value. (Warner, 1976, p. 301)

Finally, she saw Mary ascend "into the sky with a great multitude of
angels" (Warner, 1976, p. 302).

Of concern to us is that psychiatric patients with psychotic symptoms also report delusions and hallucinations with religious content.
For example, one study found that 28 percent of psychiatrically hospitalized, psychotic patients had religious delusions (Appelbaum,

Robbins, and Roth, 1999), and another found that 9 to 31 percent of them had religious auditory hallucinations (Atallah et al., 2001). When should hallucinations with religious content be regarded as psychopathological?

Before answering this question, we need to place the discussion in larger context. Many people who are not psychiatric patients report hallucinations. Ten to 15 percent of the general population reports having experienced hallucinations of some kind during their lifetime (Tien, 1991). Because only 1 percent of the population has schizophrenia (Tien, 1991), this disorder accounts for only a fraction of those reporting hallucinations. People with other disorders, such as schizotypal personality disorder or dissociative disorders, may report hallucinations because they have poor "reality discrimination," which is the ability to distinguish "the real and the imaginary" (Bentall, 1990, p. 88). Many professionals believe that this ability to discriminate reality falls on a continuum in which severe mental illness is "the extreme endpoint of a continuum of personality" (Bentall, 2000, p. 90). This could be called a continuum of "schizotypy" or "psychosis-proneness," which ranges "from normality at one end, through eccentricity and different combinations of schizotypal characteristics, to florid psychosis at the other" (Johns and van Os, 2001, p. 1132). Some who report religious visual or auditory hallucinations may lie in the psychosis-prone part of this spectrum, often without having a history of psychiatric treatment.

Of course, even normal people without any proneness to psychosis can hallucinate under stressful conditions (Bentall, 1990). For example, people can hallucinate when faced with events such as "loss of a spouse and potentially life-threatening situations" such as "mining accidents, sustained military operations, and terrorist attacks" (Bentall, 1990, p. 84).

Most important, hallucinations with religious content must be understood within their culture of origin. Bentall (1990) cites cross-cultural studies indicating that "hallucinations may be a relatively common and positively valued experience in some societies" (p. 83). An anthropological study of 488 societies worldwide (Bourguignon, 1970, cited in Bentall, 2000) showed that "hallucinations play a role in ritual practices in 62% of cultures studied" (Bentall, 2000, p. 96). In most of these cultures "hallucinations were not induced by the ingestion of psychoactive chemicals, were positively valued, and could be understood in the context of local beliefs and practices" (Bentall, 2000, p. 96). Because religion is part of culture, a key question is whether a given client's religious hallucinations are consistent with those of other followers of that religion.

As this brief review indicates, then, many people who experience religious visions are not psychotic. They may be schizotypal, dissociative, or eccentric; may be reacting to a highly stressful event; and/or may be experiencing what is expected within their religious subculture.

### Clinical Guidelines

What guidelines should we follow in determining how normal versus psychopathological a religious hallucination is? In determining whether hallucinations with religious content are psychopathological, the clinician obviously needs to do a comprehensive assessment. Such would include asking whether the patient is experiencing other hallucinations with nonreligious content and evaluating the patient for DSM-IV criteria for schizophrenia, including delusions, incoherent speech, disorganized behavior, negative symptoms, and impairment in social and occupational functioning.

Another consideration is whether the person finds the hallucinations distressing or threatening. Devoutly religious people experiencing vivid encounters with religious figures such as Mary or Jesus often describe these as affirming and positive. By contrast, many psychotic patients find their hallucinations critical and threatening. Supporting this guideline is research comparing mystical and schizophrenic experiences (studies cited by Wulff, 2000). This research shows that "positive visual hallucinations" are more often associated with mystical experience, as opposed to "negative auditory ones," which were more typical of psychosis (Wulff, 2000, p. 412).

A final consideration is whether these experiences are consistent with the teachings and rituals of the client's religious tradition. To the extent that they deviate from such, the clinician should weight them as potentially psychopathological. Consulting with the patient's minister or other religious leader could help to clarify whether it falls within that religion's range of expected religious experiences.

## CONCLUSION

Using a client-centered approach to assess spirituality is a major theme of this book. The assessment methods described in this chapter are simply ways of giving clients a mouthpiece for describing what they believe and practice, and how that relates to their coping. When we listen carefully to their views of these issues, we then have an expanded framework with which to plan effective interventions. Before I discuss interventions, however, I pause to focus on ethical issues, which is the topic of Chapter 3.

# Chapter 3

# Ethical Issues in Spirituality and Mental Health

I have emphasized the importance of taking a client-centered approach to integrating spirituality into assessment and intervention. In the assessment section I described client-centered approaches in which we invite clients to teach us about their beliefs and practices and how these help them to cope. In this chapter, too, I use a client-centered approach to discuss ethical issues in integrating spirituality into clinical work. I first summarize American Psychological Association ethical guidelines that are relevant to the issues, concluding that a client-centered approach harmonizes with these. I then discuss three difficult ethical issues that arise in clinical practice, with clinical examples.

## AMERICAN PSYCHOLOGICAL ASSOCIATION ETHICAL GUIDELINES

I believe much convergence can be seen in the ethical guidelines of the mental health professions, including those of psychiatry, psychology, clinical social work, and counseling. Therefore, although many of my readers are not psychologists, for the purpose of this discussion I draw on the guidelines of my own organization, the American Psychological Association.

The practice guidelines of American Psychological Association (1993) emphasize the importance of accounting for religious beliefs and values. They state:

> Psychologists respect client religious and/or spiritual beliefs and values, including attributions and taboos, since they affect world view, psychosocial functioning and expressions of dis-

tress. . . . Effective psychological intervention may be aided by consultation and/or inclusion of religious/spiritual leaders/practitioners relevant to the client's cultural and belief systems. (pp. 46-47)

Similarly, the multicultural guidelines of the American Psychological Association (2003) include religious/spiritual orientation as an important dimension to account for in practice. In intervening with clients, they encourage psychologists to "seek out community leaders, change agents, and influential individuals (ministers, store owners, nontraditional healers, natural helpers) when appropriate, enlisting their assistance with clients as part of a total family or community-centered (healing) approach" (American Psychological Association, 2003, p. 392).

The American Psychological Association Ethics Code (American Psychological Association, 2002) also emphasizes the importance of respecting human differences, including religious ones. They also underscore why, when dealing with religious clients, seeking consultation may be very important: psychologists must practice "only within the boundaries of their competence" (American Psychological Association, 2002, p. 1063). Consequently, where clinicians are not familiar with a client's religious approach, they may need to refer to or consult with knowledgeable clergy or colleagues, or educate themselves so that they can better work with the client.

## A CLIENT-CENTERED ETHICAL FRAMEWORK

Recently, mental health professionals have become much more sympathetic to the importance of spirituality in the lives of their clients. In the past clinicians often ignored or worked around clients' religious values. In the past decade the pendulum has swung in the opposite direction: many clinicians now have great enthusiasm for integrating spirituality into therapeutic work. One of the reasons for this swing is research showing that religious activity has positive associations with physical and mental health, though these associations do not prove that religion *causes* better health (see reviews by Powell, Shahabi, and Thoresen, 2003; Smith, McCullough, and Poll, 2003; and Ellison and Levin, 1998). Because of this consistent association, the media and medical professionals may lead people to believe that if they are not currently religious, they should become so in order to improve their health, similar to taking another vitamin. Such is a gross overinterpretation and misapplication of the empirical findings.

One problem with this swinging of the pendulum is that it can go too far in the opposite direction. For example, Chirban (2001) notes that some in the medical field have become so enamored with spirituality that they advocate clinicians' actively helping patients to increase their use of religion. They quote one publication suggesting that clinicians ask, "What can I do to support your faith or religious commitment?" Chirban (2001) argues that taking such a stance implies that "the clinician is knowledgeable and trained to 'support' the patient's religious commitment," which may not be true. Another problem is that this approach may "cross the line of professional responsibility" from the mental health arena to the "religious field" (Chirban, 2001, p. 278).

So where is the middle ground? I believe the middle ground is to take a client-centered approach, one supported by Chirban (2001). He suggests a better question to ask clients: "How can we understand your problem in view of your faith?" (Chirban, 2001, p. 278), an approach that I advocated in the previous chapter. By asking about spiritual issues in the first or second session, the clinician invites spirituality into the dialogue, letting clients know that they can talk about it freely when they wish. The litmus test then becomes the following question: "Does the patient feel free to share concerns, feelings, or experiences about religious and spiritual issues?" (Chirban, 2001, p. 278).

I view this client-centered approach as the middle ground in a continuum, as shown in Figure 3.1. On one extreme are those who ignore clients' spirituality. At the other are those who actively encourage clients to expand their religious commitment, or to consider becoming religious if they are not. In the middle is the client-centered approach. Here, clinicians ask about spirituality but attempt to follow clients' leads as to whether they wish to expand their spiritual pursuits. This is not to say that a clinician can never ask about whether a nonreligious client has considered exploring spirituality. For example, if a client appears to be searching for meaning and direction, a clinician could explore various ways that the client could do this on his or her own. However, there is a difference between this approach, in which spiri-

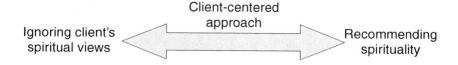

FIGURE 3.1. Finding the Middle Ground in Integrating Spirituality into Assessment and Therapy

tuality is gently explored as an option, and a therapist pushing clients to become religious or to deepen their religiosity.

## SPECIFIC ETHICAL ISSUES

Many specific ethical questions can arise in treating religious patients. Here, I address three of those: handling differences in values, modifying "destructive" religious beliefs, and praying with patients.

### Acknowledging Differences in Values

Mental health professionals and clients may hold fundamentally different moral views about issues that are relevant to the presenting problems. Examples include "the right to die, abortion, religion, drug use, and various types of sexual behavior" (Richards, Rector, and Tjeltveit, 1999, p. 149). Richards, Rector, and Tjeltveit (1999) point out that these differences are necessarily problematic but emphasize that they must be addressed appropriately. When faced with serious differences in values such as these, they recommend that therapists discuss these differences explicitly and not try to remain neutral and objective. Therapists should "openly acknowledge" these differences "while also affirming their clients' right to disagree with them" (p. 149). Then, therapists can explore "whether the value difference will undermine trust or otherwise prevent them from helping the clients pursue their therapeutic goal" (p. 149).

Obviously, this is a very general recommendation. In many situations differences in values are modest rather than extreme. In these situations we need to use our best judgment about when to explicitly discuss these differences.

## *Modifying "Destructive" Religious Beliefs*

Religious clients may hold beliefs that, in the clinician's view, compound their emotional distress or their avoidance of active problem solving. Several examples can be given. In Chapter 2 I described the problem of "scrupulosity," in which clients have perfectionistic moral standards for themselves that can never be attained. Others may have moral beliefs that cause them to behave self-destructively, such as staying with an abusive spouse (Johnson, Ridley, and Nielsen, 2000). Some may have "false expectations of God," such as having a problem-free life (Johnson, Ridley, and Nielsen, 2000, p. 16). Still others may see relying on God as a complete solution, one that causes them to "avoid reality and responsibility" (Johnson, Ridley, and Nielsen, 2000, p. 16).

How should clinicians proceed when clients hold beliefs that seem to compound their problems? Johnson, Ridley, and Nielsen (2000) emphasize that, on one hand, we must respect our clients' religious beliefs and their right to hold them. On the other hand, we "should not accept destructive religious beliefs for the sake of embracing diversity" (Johnson, Ridley, and Nielsen, 2000, p. 16). They suggest that we pursue a middle ground in attempting to modify destructive religious beliefs.

Specifically, they recommend two possible courses of action. One is to consult with clients' clergy "for clarification of doctrine and pastoral support in the treatment process" (Johnson, Ridley, and Nielsen, 2000, p. 16). This approach is particularly helpful when the client holds "idiosyncratic or inaccurate religious beliefs" that can be "appropriately corrected from within his or her faith community" (Johnson, Ridley, and Nielsen, 2000, p. 16). Of course, not all clergy are effective in helping with such. Thus, clinicians must "exercise discretion in the selection of clergy with whom they collaborate" (Johnson, Ridley, and Nielsen, 2000, p. 16). A second recommendation applies to clinicians who share or completely understand the client's religious frame of reference. Here, the clinician can attempt to modify the "demanding and evaluative nature" of these beliefs without "disputing specific religious beliefs" (Johnson, Ridley, and Nielsen, 2000, p. 16). The authors acknowledge that walking this fine line between respecting and challenging destructive beliefs is "a formidable challenge" (Johnson, Ridley, and Nielsen, 2000, p. 16).

I believe that these are two good guidelines. However, with regard to modifying clients' beliefs, clinicians should use great caution before assuming that they know enough to do this. They should do this only if they have a comprehensive understanding of the client's religious perspective. Even within one religion many diverse teachings and interpretations of scriptures can often be found. In order to modify a client's beliefs, clinicians may need to be aware of the range of teachings about certain issues that exist within the client's religion. In many cases clinicians are not familiar enough with a client's belief system to offer such an overview and are better off consulting with clergy or other clinicians who follow that religion or denomination.

## Case Example

A colleague shared with me this example of consulting with clergy about a psychotherapy client. An elderly Episcopalian man presented for psychotherapy for severe depression. He was depressed in part because he believed he would go to hell for past misdeeds, including physical abuse of his wife and not having loved his sons the way he would have wanted. The psychologist carefully assessed his religiosity and discovered that his Episcopal priest visited him weekly, but that he had never told the priest about his past misdeeds and his fear of going to hell. The psychologist did not share the client's religious perspective and thus chose not to attempt to modify his beliefs on her own. Instead, she obtained a release to talk with the priest, who agreed to a few conjoint sessions with the client and her. During those sessions the client talked with the priest about his fears of hell and punishment, which the priest challenged. As a result, he was able to reduce his guilt and self-condemnation about his past, and he no longer believed that he was going to hell. Instead of focusing on the past, he decided to focus on the present and to show as much love as he could to his sons and granddaughter. This shift in focus from regrets about the past to present-centered action was a very helpful one for him which relieved much of his depression.

## *Praying with Clients*

Surveys have shown that some mental health professionals do pray with clients in sessions, though the practice is "relatively rare" (Richards and Bergin, 1997, p. 204). I personally do not do so, and my clients have not asked to pray with me, with the exception of the case example that follows.

I agree with the stance of Richards and Bergin (1997), who have "serious reservations" about praying with clients. As they state, such may increase "the risk that role boundaries will become confused," because clients may not be clear about the "differences between the role of professional therapists and religious leaders" (Richards and Bergin, 1997, p. 204). They also raise the possibility of triggering "unhealthy transference issues" during prayer, particularly with clients "who have unresolved issues of anger toward or dependency on God and religious authorities" and thus may "project these onto the therapist" (Richards and Bergin, 1997, p. 204). At the same time, Richards and Bergin (1997) stop short of saying that therapists should never pray with clients. They believe that prayer may be appropriate for therapists practicing in religiously oriented clinics or settings, where therapists and clients share the same religious orientation. Here, therapists "may find that it is expected, comfortable, and helpful to pray with clients individually or in group sessions" (Richards and Bergin, 1997, p. 204).

*Case Example*

A patient had just died suddenly on the nursing home ward. The patients who knew him needed a brief meeting to discuss their grief and shock about his passing. I began the meeting by informing them of his passing. After some discussion, a devoutly Christian man spoke up, stating that he wanted to say a prayer for his deceased friend and to send good thoughts his way. I responded, "Let's take a moment of silence for that." We then took a minute of silence, during which the patient made a silent prayer and the other patients remained silent.

*Comment:* Because this was a secular setting and other patients did not necessarily share his religious views, I did not want to invite him to pray aloud. However, it was important for him to express his grief in this way. By allowing a moment of silence, I gave him and the others permission to pray silently in their own way. Unfortunately, the nursing home's chaplain was not available to colead that meeting with me. If he had been there, I would have deferred to the chaplain's judgment about how to handle this request. In that case the chaplain might have prayed individually with the patient after the meeting or, if the patients wanted it, ended the group session with an ecumenical prayer.

## *CONCLUSION*

The ethical issues raised by religious clients can be quite challenging. I have provided some general guidelines in this chapter, the most important of which is to take a client-centered approach—one that respects clients' beliefs and protects their autonomy as much as possible. I now apply this client-centered approach to spiritually sensitive intervention, beginning with meditation.

# Chapter 4

# Meditation

In the following four chapters I focus on interventions for clients of widely varying spiritual orientations and degrees of religious commitment. I attempt to provide an overview of interventions that are broad enough to help those from all spiritual orientations, including those who may identify themselves as agnostic, nontheist, or atheist.

In this chapter I explore the use of meditation without religious content. I exclude religious content so that meditation can be taught to all clients, not just those who are religious. On the other hand, for religious clients who want to incorporate religious content, the meditation techniques are simple enough that people can easily add their own religious content.

## *BENEFITS OF MEDITATION*

Meditation can have both psychological and spiritual benefits. One primary psychological benefit is relaxation. Studies have shown that it can lower blood pressure, decrease sympathetic nervous system arousal, and decrease cortisol levels (studies cited by Barnes, Treiber, and Davis, 2001). Another psychological benefit is the development of "mindfulness," which is "to be aware of the full range of experiences that exist in the here and now" (Marlatt and Kristeller, 1999, p. 68). This awareness is cultivated through mindfulness meditation, which is designed to develop an "observing self" that watches one's thoughts and feelings as they occur, like clouds floating by in the sky. Finally, meditation may have psychospiritual benefits, such as cultivating the "sense of inner calm, harmony and transcendence often associated with spiritual growth" by bypassing our usual daily preoccupations (Marlatt and Kristeller, 1999, p. 74).

Three primary types of meditation have been developed by Eastern religions (Marlatt and Kristeller, 1999):

1. *Concentrative meditation,* in which the meditator focuses on a "specific object of attention, such as awareness of the breath" (Marlatt and Kristeller, 1999, p. 70)
2. *Mindfulness meditation,* in which the meditator focuses on any mental content as it occurs, including thoughts, feelings, and images
3. *Transcendental Meditation,* in which the meditator repeats a Sanskrit term or other religious term (e.g., "one") as the focus of the meditation

Eastern religions also have meditations that emphasize content rather than mental process alone. For example, Buddhism offers meditations designed to enhance compassion, self-love, and happiness (Hanh, 1997).

Western religions also have developed their own approaches to meditation. For example, Christian meditation may involve meditating deeply on religious beliefs or Scripture, or communing with the divine. In Christianity clear distinctions may not always be made among meditation, prayer, and communing with God. Some Christians use their own type of Transcendental Meditation, in which a Christian term is repeated aloud or silently (e.g., "maranatha").

In my clinical work I teach only the first two types of meditation, concentrative and mindfulness meditation, because they have direct applications to coping with stress. Another reason is that neither type of meditation involves religious content, which allows me to use them in secular settings with nonreligious clients and with clients from diverse religious backgrounds. However, these two approaches are flexible enough that religious clients can add their own religious content or style to them.

Some people who do not adhere to Eastern religions wonder if they can practice these two types of meditation without inadvertently practicing the beliefs of those religions. The answer is emphatically "yes": you can use them as a purely psychological technique for observing mental processes. Of course, the Eastern religions do have a philosophical rationale for using these types of meditation. For example, in Buddhism suffering is said to arise from trying to make permanent what is impermanent, that is, "when we resist the flow of life and cling to things, events, people and ideas as permanent" (Finn and Rubin, 2000, p. 321). To alleviate this suffering, Buddhists use meditation to quiet the mind by observing the transient nature of mental phenomena and the mind's desperate process of grasping (Finn and Rubin, 2000). Because of the transient nature of mental phenomena, Buddhists infer that "there is no single self which is the subject of our changing experience" (Finn and Rubin, 2000, p. 321). However, when meditating, clients do not have to incorporate this view of the self as illusory. Instead, they can simply note the transient nature of mental phenomena.

Instructions for these two types of meditation are listed in Exhibit 4.1. Concentrative meditation is listed first because it is simpler and provides a basic skill, focusing on the breath, which is needed for mindfulness meditation. Mindfulness meditation uses the breath as an anchor point but also instructs the meditator to become aware of and to label distracting mental processes. As such, concentrative meditation creates *exclusive* awareness of the breath, whereas mindfulness meditation encourages a more *inclusive* awareness of the mind's wanderings (Finn and Rubin, 2000).

## APPLICATIONS OF MINDFULNESS MEDITATION TO COPING

Mindfulness meditation can help clients to cope more effectively in at least three ways:

1. Clients can use concentrative or mindfulness meditation as another way to relax and "ground" themselves in the present moment.
2. Mindfulness meditation can help clients to develop an "observing self," one that may help them to avoid "overidentifying" with their negative thoughts and feelings (Teasdale et al., 2002). During mindfulness meditation the "observing self" notices the transient nature of mental phenomena—that thoughts, feelings, images, and sensations all come and go. In this process they learn that their negative moods and urges are also transient and that they can just "let them pass."
3. Once they have developed this observing self, clients can learn "the use of focused but detached awareness" in coping with dif-

ficult feelings and urges (Marlatt and Kristeller, 1999, p. 79). Specifically, clients learn to attend to "'just what is,' and to see events clearly without the 'excess baggage' of mental judgement or evaluation" (Marlatt and Kristeller, 1999, p. 78). When negative thoughts and feelings arise, clients can note and be aware of them, but also can see them as "just a thought" or "just a feeling" that will pass and that they do not have to act on (Marlatt and Kristeller, 1999, p. 79).

## EXHIBIT 4.1. Meditation Instructions

### Concentrative Meditation

- Fix gaze on one spot or close eyes.
- Breathe through nostrils.
- Keep clearly focused on each breath by noticing:
    —Rising and falling of the abdomen.
    —Movement of the chest.
    —The space or pause between breaths and the sensations that go with them.
    —Breath moving in and out of nostrils.
- Use mental notations as you breathe, such as "rise-fall" or "in-out," or counting "one-one, two-two. . . ."

### Mindfulness Meditation (also called Insight or Vipassana Meditation)

- Use breathing as the anchor point of your concentration.
- As thoughts, feelings, sounds, and images arise, notice them and then return to focusing on your breathing, as follows:
    —*Sounds:* Make a mental note of "hearing" and then return to the breath.
    —*Sensations/feelings:* Make a mental note of "feelings"; observe their quality and how they change; return to focusing on the breath when feelings are no longer prominent.
    —*Images:* Make a mental note of "seeing."
    —*Thoughts:* Make a mental note of "thinking," and return to focusing on the breath. Be aware of these thoughts without critically judging them.
- Do not try to make anything happen.

*Source:* Adapted from Goldstein and Kornfield, 1987.

In applying these principles to their work with substance abusers, Marlatt and Kristeller (1999) use the analogy of surfing, in which clients are taught to "surf" their urges to use substances. They describe how one of them developed this coping technique while working with a client:

> This method first arose in the course of working with a client who was trying to give up smoking. After he had quit for a week, he reported constant urges to smoke that felt like a growing ball of discomfort that was increasing in intensity to the point that he felt he would "go crazy" unless he gave in. Recalling a prior account of his reputation as a surfer during his youth, the therapist asked, "What if you could see the craving in the form of a cresting wave instead of a growing ball?" We then discussed his experience as a budding surfer. He described how he learned to keep his balance as the ocean wave swelled up beneath his surfboard and he rode the wave as it finally crested and diminished in size. He learned to keep his balance without being "wiped out" by the wave. He agreed to transfer this surfing metaphor to his meditation practice. As soon as he experienced any indication of a rising urge in his thoughts or feelings, he would direct his full attention to this growing wave while keeping his balance until the wave gradually crested and subsided. (Marlatt and Kristeller, 1999, p. 78)

Marlatt and Kristeller (1999) coined the term *urge surfing* for this approach to handling urges to use substances and other impulse-control problems. Clients carefully observe urges to use, identify them as "just feelings" or "just thoughts," and refuse to see them as compulsions to relapse. They see the urge as just another wave that will come, crest, and go.

Of course, such an approach can be readily applied to negative mood states and could be called "mood surfing." Rather than seeing depression, anxiety, anger, or other unpleasant emotions as something they must immediately get rid of, clients can "surf the mood" by watching it come and watching it go.

In describing mindfulness applications to coping, I find it helpful to contrast them with active coping strategies. The contrast between these two approaches is displayed in Figure 4.1. On the right side of the continuum are strategies for actively reducing distress. These in-

"Letting it pass"                                    Actively reducing
(mindfulness)                                        distress

FIGURE 4.1. Actively Reducing Distress versus "Letting it Pass"

clude methods such as cognitive restructuring, engaging in pleasant events, positive distraction, seeking support from others, and taking prescribed medication. On the other side of the continuum is the very different strategy of letting it pass, which is suggested by mindfulness approaches. Here, the person makes no direct effort to lower distress, but the net result may be the same. Although these two approaches are opposite in nature, they are not opposing. In fact, they can be used in a complementary way. For example, active ways of reducing distress are usually only partly successful. Mindfulness strategies can be used to address the remaining difficult emotion.

## MINDFULNESS-BASED PSYCHOTHERAPY

Theorists have developed a method of psychotherapy based on mindfulness, called *mindfulness-based cognitive therapy* (Segal, Williams, and Teasdale, 2002). As one would expect, mindfulness meditation is a foundational part of this therapy. In addition, therapists encourage clients to develop closely related skills, such as present centeredness, in which clients are taught to deal with the immediate situation rather than the past or future (Bishop, 2002). Another therapeutic goal is to develop a general attitude of nonstriving and acceptance (Bishop, 2002). Mindfulness therapists believe this is important because depression and anxiety are often made worse by the person's desperate, ruminative, and habitual attempts to escape negative mood or create positive feelings. Thus, clients are taught to let go of these desperate attempts and to expand awareness and acceptance of "what is," including negative thoughts and feelings (Segal, Williams, and Teasdale, 2002). In acquiring these skills, clients hopefully learn disidentification, or "metacognitive awareness," which is the capacity to avoid "overidentifying" with one's negative thoughts by stepping back and observing them as a spectator (Teasdale et al., 2002). Many other applications of mindfulness have been made to psychotherapy (see Baer, 2003, and Kabat-Zinn, 2003, for reviews).

## *Efficacy of Mindfulness Applications to Psychotherapy*

How effective these applications are is uncertain because empirical research on the effectiveness of mindfulness in psychotherapy is just beginning. Studies have often lacked control groups (Bishop, 2002) or have methodological problems (Baer, 2003). However, some evidence supports the importance of metacognitive awareness in reducing depression. For example, a recent study showed that increased metacognitive ability is associated with less vulnerability to depression and less vulnerability to depressive relapse (Teasdale et al., 2002). Furthermore, Teasdale and colleagues (2002) point out that outcome studies of cognitive therapy do not show that clients endorse dysfunctional thoughts less after therapy than before, which runs contrary to the expectations of cognitive therapy theory. They believe that cognitive therapy works primarily because it teaches clients to see "negative experiences as mental events in a wider context or field of awareness" (Teasdale et al., 2002, p. 276).

## CONCLUSION

Perhaps more than any other religious practice, meditation integrates spirituality and mental health. The spiritual and psychological benefits of meditation are not easily separated, nor need they be. Over the next decade, it will be exciting to see what new applications of meditation are created for clinical practice. Equally exciting may be the findings of social scientists who are researching the role of meditation in creating and sustaining positive emotions and adaptive behavior (see Goleman, 2003, for an overview). I now turn to other spiritually attuned interventions for clients with specific problems.

Chapter 5

# Letting Go of Anger
# and Practicing Forgiveness

In recent years mental health professionals have begun to use forgiveness as an intervention with clients who have anger about past offenses. Although professionals have always helped clients to "let go of anger," therapists have now begun to use the word *forgiveness*. Many provide a secular, therapeutic rationale for using it, rather than one rooted in a religious or twelve-step tradition.

I include a lengthy discussion of forgiveness here for three other reasons. First, many of our clients come to us living in a prison of rage, resentment, and hurt over past offenses. They are desperate for liberation. Second, in addressing their need for liberation, many mental health professionals and the media have emphasized forgiveness as the key. Forgiveness is often presented to them as a panacea, without acknowledging its complexity and the ambivalence many of them feel about forgiving. I hope to provide a balanced, cautious view of the issues. Third, many religious clients come to us with forgiveness as an ideal that their religions encourage them to pursue. Whether they initiate using the word "forgiveness" or not, it may be something they are considering or that they feel they *should* do even if they have not been able to do so. In such cases, we should be prepared to help them evaluate their choices about forgiving and to examine their possible guilt about not doing so.

## *FORGIVENESS AS A RELIGIOUS PRINCIPLE*

Forgiveness is a practice recommended by religions of the world and the twelve-step tradition of Alcoholics Anonymous. Each supports forgiveness in the ways noted in Exhibit 5.1. The twelve-step

**EXHIBIT 5.1. Teachings About Forgiveness
in World Religions and the Twelve Steps**

- *Judaism:* God forgives and thus we should also.

- *Christianity:* God's forgiveness of human sins is a central teaching. Christians should imitate God's forgiveness: "Forgive us our debts as we forgive our debtors" (Matthew 6:12).

- *Islam:* Allah forgives and the Prophet Muhammad practiced forgiveness. Followers of Islam should practice forgiveness.

- *Buddhism:* As a religion it is dedicated to relieving suffering in all its forms. Compassion and forbearance (restraining oneself from avenging a wrong so as not to create even more suffering) are two key tools for relieving suffering. Resentment creates more suffering for oneself and possibly for others. By the law of karma, hating another may make it more likely that one will be hated by others in the future.

- *Hinduism:* For those wishing to follow the path of dharma (righteousness), forgiveness is one of the behaviors to practice. Forgiveness is modeled by various Hindu gods and goddesses. The law of karma also applies here, as in Buddhism (see above).

- *The Twelve Steps:* Forgiveness is emphasized by Steps five ("admitted our wrongs"), eight ("became willing to make amends"), and nine ("made direct amends wherever possible").

*Source:* Rye et al., 2000.

tradition emphasizes seeking forgiveness, whereas world religions underscore the importance of both forgiving others and seeking it from others and/or a deity.

However, to say that religions wholeheartedly embrace forgiveness is too simplistic. Affinito (2002) points out that religions emphasize both forgiveness and justice, and that some of their sacred texts seem to encourage punishment as a way of enforcing justice. After reviewing this mixture of teachings, she concludes that this highly controversial area offers no consensus on how to reconcile these different emphases within religious traditions.

Another problem is that religionists have often not practiced forgiveness toward those who deviate from their beliefs and morals. As Spilka and colleagues (2003) put it:

Forgiveness is most likely to apply to believers of religious systems, not to unbelievers, to outgroup members, or to "alien others." ... The religiously committed in many faiths have enslaved outsiders or even backed inhumane indentured servitude of their own coreligionists. Forgiveness on the part of either the perpetrators or victims of such inhumanity has invariably been considered irrelevant. Frequently, with the approval of church authorities, deviation from religious norms has been treated as unforgivable sin, resulting in disenfranchisement, exile, torture, and murder. (p. 171)

Because of this hypocrisy and the sometimes contradictory emphasis on justice seeking, not all religious clients may practice forgiveness or hold it as an ideal to strive for. Supporting this inference is a study of Christian older adults by Krause and Ingersoll-Dayton (2001), who found widely varying approaches to forgiveness: some said "they were always open to forgiving others"; some tended to forgive but had "reservations"; some weighed the "nature of the transgression" before deciding to forgive; and others appeared unwilling to forgive (p. 261).

## DEFINITIONS AND TYPES OF FORGIVENESS

What is forgiveness? The answer is controversial. I define forgiveness as synonymous with letting go of anger: Forgiveness is a significant decrease in negative thoughts and feelings toward a transgressor or, in the case of self-forgiveness, toward oneself.

Some forgiveness theorists would agree only partly with this definition. They would add that forgiveness involves not only a reduction in negative attitudes and feelings, but also an increase in positive feelings toward the transgressor (McCullough, Pargament, and Thoresen, 2000). For example, Enright, Freedman, and Rique (1998) define forgiveness as "a willingness to abandon one's right to resentment, negative judgment, and indifferent behavior toward one who unjustly hurt us, while fostering the undeserved qualities of compassion, generosity, and even love toward him or her" (cited in McCullough, Pargament, and Thoresen, 2000, p. 8). Similarly, McCullough, Pargament, and Thoresen (2000) add a sense of reconciliation to their definition: "intraindividual, prosocial change toward a perceived transgressor that is situated within a specific interpersonal context" (p. 9). Most religions emphasize this expanded notion of forgiveness, one that involves compassion toward the offender.

I agree that sometimes forgiveness does involve "prosocial" feelings and actions toward the offender, but I do not believe that such is necessary in order to experience a complete decrease in negative thoughts and feelings about a previous offense. In fact, for reasons discussed later, I think that including such a requirement in the definition can cause some to resist forgiving. However, if a given client's definition of forgiveness involves extending compassion to an offender, then we need to accept and account for that in our work with the client.

There are four types of forgiveness:

1. Forgiving another with whom one *no longer has* a relationship
2. Forgiving another with whom one *has* an ongoing relationship
3. Seeking forgiveness from another for one's own transgressions
4. Self-forgiveness

Forgiveness protocols for psychoeducation or psychotherapy focus almost exclusively on the first two types of forgiveness, those involving the offenses of others. The twelve-step tradition emphasizes seeking forgiveness from others. I am unaware of models of self-forgiveness per se, but many therapeutic approaches address the same issue of absolving oneself of excess guilt.

## THEORETICAL PHASES OF FORGIVENESS

Various mental health professionals have developed detailed steps to forgiveness and taught these to clients. They teach these in psycho-educational groups of several weeks' duration, during which they take clients through the "steps to forgiveness." Although these steps differ from theorist to theorist, they tend to have the following key phases in common (Enright and Fitzgibbons, 2000):

- *Uncovering phase:* Acknowledging how the offense has made one's life more emotionally and behaviorally difficult. Clients may be instructed to ask themselves a motivational self-assessment question, such as: "How many rooms in your house does this resentment occupy?" (Luskin, 2002).

- *Decision phase:* Recognizing that old resolution strategies have not worked and resolving to try forgiveness.
- *Work phase:* Various therapists have described detailed steps and techniques for helping clients to move toward forgiveness. Here are four examples:
  —Gaining an empathic understanding of the offender and why the offender may have committed the offense, which may decrease clients' negative emotion about the offense.
  —Challenging clients' "unenforceable rules" that keep them holding on to resentment: e.g., "People have to treat me with kindness or care in the way that I want," or "Life should be fair" (Luskin, 2002, p. 135).
  —Viewing the offender from a broader, transcendent point of view. For example, seeing the offender in "global perspective," e.g., as a "genuine human being" who is part of the "human community," rather than "writing off" the person (Enright, 2001, p. 152). Religious clients might choose to view the offender in "cosmic perspective," e.g., seeing the person as part of the world's overall divine plan, or asking how "God sees" the offender (Enright, 2001, pp. 152-154).
  —Taking more personal responsibility. This point would apply to those who have not taken full responsibility for their role in the offense. When such people carefully reconsider an offense, they may realize that they shared much more responsibility for it than they had previously thought. Consequently, they may feel less angry with the offender. For example, a recovering substance abuser told me that for years he had blamed his brother for getting him started on hard drugs by offering them to him. However, after looking carefully at what occurred, he recalled that, prior to his brother's offer, he had been "wanting to try them for a long time," so that it was only a matter of finding an opportunity to experiment. This recognition defused much of his anger toward his brother as *the* responsible party.
- *Deepening phase:* Finding increased meaning in the suffering, deeper connection with others, and perhaps renewed purpose in life.

## Case Example

An elderly Hispanic client of mine, "Ricardo," told me how he had used empathizing with the offender to reduce his lifelong rage toward his father. After enduring heavy combat during wartime, his father had chosen not to return home, abandoning Ricardo, his mother, and siblings when he was a small boy. His mother and he never again had contact with him and never learned why his father had left them. For many years Ricardo had felt extremely angry with his father, an anger that had been reinforced by his mother's rage toward her husband. This rage and hurt had often served as a trigger for Ricardo's alcohol abuse and depression.

After twenty-five years of simmering resentment, however, he reached a turning point. His psychologist invited him to empathize with his father so that he could understand why this might have happened. The psychologist suggested that he think carefully about the trauma his father probably had suffered in the war and its impact on his father's emotional health. In doing so, Ricardo appreciated how posttraumatic stress might have driven his father to abandon close relationships, even those of his own family. This simple step brought him great relief, because he no longer assumed that his father was just an evil man who had abandoned them out of pure selfishness or spite. Although he continued to feel some anger toward his father, empathizing helped him to stop demonizing his father and to arrive at a more balanced view.

## THERAPEUTIC EFFICACY OF FORGIVENESS

Research in this area is still in the preliminary stages. However, some empirical evidence suggests that forgiveness is associated with better emotional and relational health. For example, some studies show that patients who move toward forgiving someone who has wronged them show decreases in anxiety and depression (Sanderson and Linehan, 1999, cite studies by Coyle and Enright, 1997; Freedman and Enright, 1996). For those attempting to restore strained relationships, there is evidence that "forgiveness can be an important step in restoring relationships that have been harmed through transgression" (Exline and Baumeister, 2000, p. 150). Looking on the psychopathological side of the coin, research shows that "defensive responses such as revenge fantasies and blaming have been associated with psychopathology . . . and poor health outcomes" (Exline and Baumeister, 2000, p. 134).

How effective are the "steps to forgiveness" programs? Studies have shown that psychoeducational programs can promote forgiveness. However, most have used participants from self-selected samples rather than clinical samples, so we do not know how effective they are with patients seeking treatment in traditional settings (Malcolm and Greenberg, 2000). Furthermore, the models of forgiveness and their attendant steps have not been validated (Malcolm and Greenberg, 2000). We do not know which of the steps carry the most versus least therapeutic benefit and if any steps could be discarded. For example, developing empathy for the offender may or may not be essential in order to reduce one's anger at that person. Finally, these "steps to forgiveness" programs have not been compared head-to-head with traditional psychotherapy. Thus, we are still not certain whether they are any more effective than traditional psychotherapy for helping people to reduce anger at others or themselves (Malcolm and Greenberg, 2000). Hopefully, future research will show how effective they are as compared with traditional psychotherapy.

On the other hand, I believe many people "let go of" their resentment without deliberately going through any steps. Their resentment gradually slips away, proving the adage, "Time heals." As Lamb (2002) writes,

> An individual can experience a lessening of symptoms through the natural processes of responding and reacting to wounds. . . . Sometimes a bad act loses its significance because good deeds, warmer feelings, and a sense of changed character crowd it out. Sometimes a person grows, deepens, softens, gains insight, and comes to feel differently about the offender. (p. 161)

## POTENTIAL DISADVANTAGES OF FORGIVENESS

With the current emphasis on forgiveness, it would be easy to conclude that everyone should forgive all offenses all the time. I think such an expectation is unrealistic. As clinicians, we should take a client-centered approach to forgiveness, one involving a careful assessment of someone's readiness for letting go of anger.

Faced with the option of forgiving, many clients are brought face to face with the disadvantages of letting go of their anger. Here are some of those disadvantages that the victim might perceive (Exline and Baumeister, 2000; Pargament, McCullough, and Thoresen, 2000):

- In the case of an ongoing relationship, the victim may fear that forgiveness will give the perpetrator free license to repeat the transgression, keep the victim in a destructive relationship, or make him or her appear weak or vulnerable.
- The victim may believe that justice will not be served. I discuss this difficult issue in more detail later.
- The victim may lose the benefits of victim status, such as occupying the high moral ground or having the power to induce guilt, to demand reparations, or to punish the perpetrator.

Just because, in a given case, someone perceives these disadvantages to forgiveness does not mean they are rational or reality based. However, clinicians need to understand that person's reservations about forgiveness. Knowing that their reservations are understood and accepted, clients can then engage in a process of weighing questions such as, "What are the advantages versus disadvantages of moving toward forgiveness?" and "How much would I consider forgiving the offense?"

## CONTINUUM OF FORGIVENESS

This second question—"How much would I forgive?"—brings up an important point: forgiveness need not be an "all or nothing" proposition. Some people believe that forgiveness involves ridding oneself of almost all negative feelings about the offense, whereas not forgiving involves keeping almost all the resentment. In contrast, I propose that forgiveness is a continuum, as shown in Figure 5.1. At the "no forgiveness" end of the scale, one may experience rage with accompanying revenge fantasies or plans. At the "complete forgiveness" end of the scale, one has no negative feelings when recalling the offense. In some cases this may be accompanied by reconciling with the offender; expressing positive feelings toward that person; and, in the case of ongoing relationships, believing that the wounded relationship has been "healed." However, as mentioned, I do not think that such positive feelings toward an offender are essential for complete forgiveness.

Recall that I defined forgiveness as a significant decrease in negative thoughts and feelings toward a perceived transgressor. That means that a 50 percent reduction in negative attitudes and feelings

No forgiveness

Complete forgiveness

FIGURE 5.1. Continuum of Forgiveness

could be considered 50 percent forgiveness. We could also say that one has "let go of" 50 percent of his or her anger about the offense.

What are some of the points along the continuum from "no forgiveness" to "complete forgiveness"? Many steps could be described, but I will mention five.

- Moving slightly away from the "no forgiveness" end of the scale, one could feel very angry when recalling the offense, but *without impulses to get revenge*. Wanting revenge is not necessarily the same as wanting punishment. Revenge, in contrast with punishment, may involve inflicting pain over and above that of the original offense and may be delivered directly by the ones offended, as in murdering a murderer. In these ways revenge is a more extreme and self-directed form of inflicting punishment.
- One could *protest* that the offense occurred, e.g., "that should never have happened to me," but without as much anger.
- One could *accept* that the offense occurred, without constantly protesting it every time one recalls it. Here the person might also attempt to "channel" his or her anger in a constructive direction when recalling the offense. For example, one could take determined steps to prevent it from recurring, support others who have been similarly victimized, or, in the case of offenders who are being legally prosecuted, decide to accept the court's decision about punishment for the offender.
- One could *neutralize* memories of the offense by learning to ignore them when they arise. For example, a woman in one of my classes mentioned that a friend of hers was murdered, and she found herself very angry with the man who did it. Although she decided she did not want to forgive this man, she did find that she was able simply to set aside memories of the murder when they came to mind, thus disarming them.

- One could *develop empathy* for the offender yet decide not to forgive the offense completely. That is, one could make an effort to understand why the offender might have done the deed but decide not to let go of some anger toward the person. Lamb (2002) calls this "compassion without forgiveness" (p. 162), and encourages clinicians to accept clients' ambivalence and complex mix of feelings. She asks rhetorically, "Can't a wronged person feel both resentment and compassion?" (Lamb, 2002, p. 162).

As clients consider a given offense, it may be helpful for them to identify where on the continuum of forgiveness they are. In some cases they may find that they have partially let go of the offense without realizing it. They can then evaluate whether they want to move further toward the forgiveness end of the scale. Those who want to do so can use some of the "steps to forgiveness" or other methods to move more toward the positive end of the scale. Some may wish to read self-help books on forgiveness.

### *Case Example*

In my psychoeducational spirituality group (Chapter 7) I have a section on forgiveness. In teaching this section with outpatient substance abusers in early recovery, I found that most could identify offenses from the past that they were still very angry about. I then asked them to say whether they wanted to move toward forgiving the offenses. Some admitted that they were so incensed by the offenses that they would not consider "letting them go." For example, some of them had had physically abusive fathers, with whom they were so angry that they did not want to consider forgiving them. When they admitted such feelings to the group, some of their peers became alarmed, saying that their staying angry about these offenses would serve as a trigger for future relapse on substances. In these instances I had to rein in the group's pressure to forgive. Instead, I empathized with the difficulty these clients were having in forgiving the offense and emphasized that they have every right to remain angry if they wished. However, I also suggested that after the group they consider taking a careful "emotional inventory" of the offense in which they asked themselves questions such as, "What price have I paid for hanging on to this anger?"; "What are the advantages and disadvantages of holding on to it?"; and "Do I want to let go of any part of my anger?" After reflecting on such questions, they could then consider sharing their answers with a therapist or peers for feedback.

*Comment:* This scenario underscores the importance of not pressuring clients to forgive. Obviously, pressuring them to forgive may create only more resistance to doing so. Even if they do forgive under pressure, their forgiveness may be superficial and half-hearted, leaving them with no long-term reduction in resentment.

## *THE CONTINUING CONTROVERSY OVER FORGIVENESS*

This growing emphasis on forgiveness as a psychotherapeutic technique has spawned a backlash of caution and challenges. These are well summarized in a book, *Before Forgiving: Cautionary Views of Forgiveness in Psychotherapy* (Lamb and Murphy, 2002). A few of the cautions and controversies from this book are summarized next.

### *Severity of the Offense*

Lamb (2002) argues that some crimes are too terrible to consider forgiving, citing the example of the Holocaust. Underscoring the importance of this point is the previously cited study by Krause and Ingersoll-Dayton (2001), who found that some Christian older adults "felt that some offenses were so egregious that forgiveness simply was not possible" (p. 259).

Lamb (2002) notes a book edited by Simon Wiesenthal (1976), who poses the question of whether a Jewish concentration camp prisoner should accept a dying Nazi guard's request for forgiveness. Some of the authors "advocate forgiveness for the peace of mind of the Jew or for the greater good of civilization," while others "say that the suffering of the Jews was so great, the damage so huge, and the crime so horrific that it is understandable why a Jew would never forgive" (Lamb, 2002, p. 155).

### *Unrepentant Offenders*

In the previous example, the Nazi guard is asking forgiveness. However, many perpetrators do not apologize or seek forgiveness. Some deny or minimize the offense, and others are too proud to ask forgiveness. I believe that in these cases forgiveness is very difficult for victims, especially when the offenses are severe and create ongoing loss or harm.

The previously cited study by Krause and Ingersoll-Dayton (2001) also bolsters the importance of this issue. Some of their Christian older adults believed

> that before transgressors can be forgiven, they must take one or more of the following steps: (1) they must be aware of what they have done; (2) explicitly ask for forgiveness; (3) offer an explanation; (4) make a resolution not to repeat the offense; (5) change their behavior; and (6) make amends. (Krause and Ingersoll-Dayton, 2001, p. 263)

Lamb (2002) believes that the problem of unrepentant offenders is particularly relevant for abused women who have suffered rape, spousal abuse, or childhood sexual abuse. In these cases the perpetrator rarely apologizes or asks forgiveness and often completely denies the crime. She argues that forgiveness is unrealistic in these cases if it involves "not only the giving up of resentment, hatred, or anger, but also the taking up a stance of love and compassion, even when the forgiver understands that the offender has no right to such benevolence" (Lamb, 2002, p. 157). She fears that "opening the heart" to an unrepentant offender comes too close to excusing the offense (Lamb, 2002). I have attempted to avoid this problem in my definition of forgiveness by including only the decrease in negative emotion and not the development of positive emotion toward the offender.

In my own clinical practice I have found that both men and women with histories of abuse often face an enormous struggle when it comes to "letting go" of anger toward an unrepentant, and often deceased, offender. They may find it completely repugnant to think about empathizing or reconciling with the offender. With such clients it is particularly advantageous to define forgiveness as I have, that is, without requiring a prosocial change toward the offender. With all clients I use the previously stated strategy, in which I invite them to consider where they are on the "resentment scale" and to think about whether and how they want to make incremental movement toward less anger. To make such small movement, for example, they might choose to retain some anger toward the offender even while expressing some empathy and compassion.

## Women and Forgiveness

Continuing her discussion of women abused by unrepentant perpe-trators, Lamb (2002) objects to pressuring them to forgive, because such pressure plays into "deep stereotypes of women's 'essential' na-ture, stereotypes that have been harmful to women in the past" (p. 156). One stereotypical expectation is that "women are more com-passionate" than men and thus more likely to forgive without "re-questing remorse, reparation, or damages" (Lamb, 2002, p. 166). This expectation may be reinforced by mental health professionals, who tend to view angry and resentful women as unhealthy (studies cited by Lamb, 2002). Instead of expecting these women to forgive, she suggests (1) assuring them that "forgiveness is only one of many options"; (2) portraying anger and resentment as natural human re-sponses that are "acceptable and not a stage through which one passes"; and (3) where necessary, helping them to "live with their an-ger and resentment" (Lamb, 2002, p. 168).

## Justice

Victims may experience a very strong tension between the impulse to forgive and the desire for justice. Such tension is understandable for three reasons. First, as mentioned previously, religions often em-phasize both justice seeking through punishment as well as forgive-ness, a tension not easily resolved. Second, wanting punishment for an offense is natural. Third, our legal system is built on the principle of "retributive justice," which takes "a reciprocity-based, eye for an eye approach, with little, if any, room for mercy toward the perpetra-tor" (Exline and Baumeister, 2000, p. 146). Its assumption is that of-fenders must not be forgiven but instead must be "brought to justice" by "making them pay for their crimes" so that the "scales of justice" are righted. Although such an approach may not act as a deterrent for actual crime, the majority of people appear to want criminals pun-ished.

By contrast, forgiveness "often requires the loosening of justice standards in order to permit mercy" (Exline and Baumeister, 2000, p. 147). Some of those encouraging forgiveness ignore this issue of how immoral behavior should be addressed when community stan-dards of morality are violated. To the extent that forgiveness ignores immoral behavior, it may "discount" the offender "as an ethical human being" accountable to community laws and moral codes (Affinito, 2002, p. 101).

In the context of psychotherapy, there is no consensus on how to account for this issue of justice seeking. I can only emphasize the importance of taking a client-centered approach to helping clients consider forgiveness. On a cognitive level, we should invite clients to tell us their beliefs about forgiveness, justice seeking, and punishment. On an emotional level, we need to hear their rage about the offense. This does not mean that we necessarily support their taking any action against the offender. As Affinito (2002) states:

> Room should be made for the client to spend the rage in talk and fantasy for the time being—to postpone action until there has been an opportunity to explore all options. The goal is to reduce the obsessive rage or resentment sufficiently so that the client can move on to a more cognitive, decision making perspective. (p. 104)

### My Personal View

I present the previous points to illustrate the complexity of the issues raised by the forgiveness movement. No easy answers address these dilemmas and controversies. Personally, I believe in a time to forgive, a time not to forgive, and a time to partly forgive. I have not been able to arrive at clear guidelines for when each is appropriate, because in most situations, "it all depends." Ideally, in my clinical work I strive to take a client-centered approach to forgiveness, helping clients decide how much anger to let go of, if any, and when and how to do it.

## SELF-FORGIVENESS

I define self-forgiveness as a decrease in negative thoughts and emotions toward oneself about a harmful mistake or offense one has made. Here again, a continuum of forgiveness can be used, as in Figure 5.2, with "no self-forgiveness" and "complete self-forgiveness" as the poles. At its most extreme, "no self-forgiveness" may involve self-hatred or self-punishment (e.g., suicide attempts or self-mutilation).

No self-forgiveness                    Complete self-forgiveness

FIGURE 5.2. Continuum of Self-Forgiveness

At the "complete self-forgiveness" end of the scale, one may experience healthy remorse, or healthy remorse coupled with resolve to compensate for the damage one did, either by making amends to the victim or by making positive contributions to the lives of others (i.e., "giving back").

Between these two points, we can imagine graduated points as we move from the "no self-forgiveness" pole to the "complete self-forgiveness" pole. Such points could be harsh self-criticism, moderate self-criticism, and acceptance that one committed the offense with only mild self-criticism. Clinicians can show clients the continuum of self-forgiveness and describe some of the points along it. They can encourage them to identify where they are on this scale for any given offense of theirs. If clients want to move further toward self-forgiveness, the clinician and they can explore strategies for doing so.

The twelve-step tradition offers one way of encouraging self-forgiveness. This approach emphasizes asking for forgiveness from others. Specifically, the process involves taking "a fearless moral inventory of ourselves" (Step 4); admitting "to God, to ourselves, and to another human being the exact nature of our wrongs" (Step 5); making "a list of all persons we had harmed" (Step 8); and making "direct amends to such people wherever possible" (Step 9). When they acknowledge past offenses, seek forgiveness, and make restitution, twelve-step members often experience self-forgiveness.

I know of no psychotherapists who have proposed "steps to self-forgiveness," as they have for forgiving others. However, each system of psychotherapy has its own way of addressing this issue. For example, in cognitive-behavioral therapy and rational-emotive therapy, clinicians ask clients to challenge cognitive distortions or irrational thoughts that fuel destructive self-criticism and unhealthy guilt. Having perfectionistic expectations of oneself is an example of a distortion that can contribute to unresolved guilt.

For religious clients, clinicians should ask about their spiritual perspective on self-forgiveness. For example, Judaism and Christianity teach that God forgives those who "repent." Most religions have rituals, such as confession to a priest or God, that their followers can use to obtain forgiveness. In some instances clients endorse these beliefs and go through these rituals yet still do not feel released from their "burden of guilt." In these cases clinicians can explore the reasons for this and account for those in planning interventions.

## Case Example

The patient was a middle-aged man who was recovering from a long history of severe cocaine dependence. He had made numerous suicidal gestures and a few serious attempts at suicide, all of which occurred while using cocaine. Asked what, aside from cocaine, triggered his suicide attempts, he said that memories of a past offense often triggered severe depression and a desire to punish himself. Specifically, during a period in which he was living with his cousins, he introduced them to cocaine and got them addicted to it. Even in his recovery program he continued to feel extremely self-critical about this. He was frustrated that they had also refused to communicate with him after this, despite his efforts to apologize.

I showed him the continuum of self-forgiveness described previously, noting that he was at the "no self-forgiveness" end of the continuum. I pointed out that currently memories of the offense were leading him to "self-punishment," and wrote that term at that end of the continuum. I then showed him some of the points along the continuum. To the right of "self-punishment" I wrote "self-condemnation without self-punishment"; to the right of that I wrote "self-criticism without self-condemnation"; and to the right of that I wrote "mild self-criticism with remorse." I distinguished between the unhealthy, self-destructive guilt he was currently feeling and a healthy, remorseful guilt that he might move toward. I pointed out that he could use this healthy remorse to strengthen his resolve to make positive contributions to the lives of others during his recovery. That is, if he could not make amends with his cousins, perhaps he could give to others "in their name."

I suggested that he write a letter to his cousins that he would not necessarily mail, one in which he expressed his apologies and remorse. Unfortunately, after doing this he felt even angrier with himself and was reminded of his frustration with their not having responded to his previous attempts at reconciliation. He did not want to risk mailing the letter and having them ignore it, which he would have interpreted as just one more sign that they had cut off communication for good. I then suggested that he write a letter of self-forgiveness to himself about the offense, in which he acknowledged the severity of his addiction at the time, expressed remorse about what happened, and resolved to use the memories of this incident to motivate his "giving back" during his recovery. After writing this, he expressed emotional relief, believing that he had taken a small step away from destructive guilt and toward healthy remorse.

*Comment:* This case illustrates the difficulty in forgiving oneself for having done something very damaging, especially when the victim does not want to receive apologies or requests for forgiveness. However, even small steps toward the self-forgiveness end of the scale can be helpful. The case also illustrates how I try to balance self-forgiveness with an honest recognition of one's offenses and their consequences, which can lead to healthy remorse.

## CONCLUSION

Forgiveness is an enormously complex and controversial issue. My intention in this chapter has been to provide you with an overview of these issues, so that you can refine your own thinking and clinical approach in this area. Hopefully, in the next decade empirical studies will shed light on some of the key issues, providing more specific guidance for clinical work.

# Chapter 6

# Spiritually Attuned Intervention

In this chapter I provide guidance on intervention with three client groups: those with substance abuse problems, those encountering trauma or life crisis, and those who are devoutly religious. Although spiritual perspectives apply to many other types of presenting problems, I think they are especially relevant to these areas.

## SUBSTANCE-ABUSING CLIENTS: THE TWELVE-STEP TRADITION

Why is it important for clinicians to understand the spiritual philosophy of the twelve steps? First, many clients will have had experience with twelve-step groups and endorse their "beliefs, values and practices" (Tonigan, Toscova, and Connors, 1999, p. 112). Second, clinicians may wish to refer clients to twelve-step groups because of possible treatment efficacy. As Tonigan, Toscova, and Connors (1999) observe:

> Correlational research suggests that 12-step participation is associated with reductions in targeted behavior, such as drinking, illicit drug use, or overeating. Likewise, membership in 12-step programs has been associated with improved psychosocial functioning and increased commitment to change, and it may offset the influence of unsupportive social networks. (p. 112)

### Key Spiritual Components of the Twelve-Step Tradition

The twelve steps of Alcoholics Anonymous are listed in Exhibit 6.1. An asterisk has been placed beside the five steps with explicitly religious content. Tonigan, Toscova, and Connors (1999) note that

**EXHIBIT 6.1. The Twelve Steps of Alcoholics Anonymous**

1. We admitted we were powerless over alcohol—that our lives had become unmanageable.
*2. Came to believe that a Power greater than ourselves could restore us to sanity.
*3. Made a decision to turn our will and our lives over to the care of God *as we understood Him.*
4. Made a searching and fearless moral inventory of ourselves.
5. Admitted to God, to ourselves, and to another human being the exact nature of our wrongs.
*6. Were entirely ready to have God remove all these defects of character.
*7. Humbly asked Him to remove our shortcomings.
8. Made a list of all persons we had harmed, and became willing to make amends to them all.
9. Made direct amends to such people wherever possible, except when to do so would injure them or others.
10. Continued to take personal inventory and when we were wrong promptly admitted it.
*11. Sought through prayer and meditation to improve our conscious contact with God *as we understood Him,* praying only for knowledge of His will for us and the power to carry that out.
12. Having a spiritual awakening as the result of these steps, we tried to carry this message to alcoholics, and to practice these principles in all our affairs.

*Source:* Alcoholics Anonymous, 1976.

*Explicitly religious steps.

steps one to three emphasize a "deferring relationship with a higher power"; that steps four to ten involve "self-examination, disclosure, and making amends to harmed persons"; and that steps eleven and twelve foster a "collaborative relationship with a higher power" (p. 118). In addition, Tonigan, Toscova, and Connors (1999) summarize key spiritual components of the twelve-step approaches:

- *Identifying a higher power, or transcendent being:* The definition of such power is left to the individual, so that a deity need not necessarily be chosen. For example, I knew a man who did not believe in God but chose "Mother Nature" as his higher power. I also knew an agnostic woman who said that she used a group of her friends as her higher power. When she was having difficulty, she would imagine her friends sitting with her, supporting and advising her.
- *A personal relationship with the higher power:* Because the individual is seen as powerless over the addiction, the higher power serves as the primary source of strength for preventing relapse. The individual communes with the higher power through prayer and meditation.
- *Sobriety is achieved through miraculous intervention by the higher power:* The higher power has accomplished what the addict could not.
- *Daily renewal of spiritual practice:* "Spirituality has neither a past nor a future for AA members. In essence, spirituality is only experienced in the present tense and may evaporate at any moment yet be restored as quickly" (Tonigan, Toscova, and Connors, 1999, p. 119).
- *Serenity:* Twelve-step programs emphasize the importance of serenity as a "core component, outcome, or both of the recovery process" (Connors, Toscova, and Tonigan, 1999, p. 237). In the twelve-step tradition an important key to serenity is acceptance of personal limitations and current circumstances. Such emphasis is epitomized by the Serenity Prayer, the first stanza of which states: "God, grant me the serenity to accept the things I cannot change, the courage to change the things I can, and the wisdom to know the difference."

## Should Only Religious Clients Be Referred to Twelve-Step Groups?

Some professionals have been reluctant to refer atheistic and nonreligious clients to twelve-step groups, because they fear that these clients will have difficulty with these groups' emphasis on a higher power. How appropriate is this concern?

Winzelberg and Humphreys (1999) did a study that sought to address this issue by asking the question: Do nonreligious substance abusers appear to benefit from twelve-step participation as much as religious substance abusers? They studied 3,000 male VA substance abuse inpatients admitted to twenty-one- to twenty-eight-day programs. The patients were given questionnaires upon admission and then twelve months after discharge. These questionnaires assessed religious behaviors and beliefs; use of substances and substance abuse–related problems; and the number of twelve-step meetings they had voluntarily attended in the past three months. Consistent with previous studies, the results at the twelve-month follow-up showed that more frequent attendance at twelve-step meetings was associated with less frequent use of substances and fewer substance abuse–related problems. More important, this association was just as strong for nonreligious patients as for religious ones.

Winzelberg and Humphreys (1999) cautiously conclude: "Although these findings await replication in other samples, . . . we suggest that clinicians at least explore the possibility of 12-step group involvement with nonreligious patients, especially where alternatives (e.g., Secular Organization for Sobriety) are not available" (p. 794). Other examples of nonreligious self-help groups are Smart Recovery and Rational Recovery.

### *Case Example*

The following case is an example of how a devoutly Christian client in recovery found the twelve steps helpful. The client was a thirty-eight-year-old homeless man participating in residential treatment for a lifelong history of alcohol and cocaine dependence. He felt humiliated that he had relapsed and become homeless again, particularly because he was a professional with a master's degree. Naturally, he was quite anxious about whether he could maintain abstinence after the program and get his life back together.

During my intake interview I asked my usual screening question about whether he had spiritual beliefs or practices that helped him cope. He responded that he had been attending a Baptist church for a few months, where he had joined a Christian AA group and practiced the twelve steps. I then gave him the Religious Beliefs and Behaviors Questionnaire and asked him about his responses. Asked about who God is for him, he stated that he believed in the Christian God and that such was his higher power. He thought often about God because his Christian twelve-step group emphasized that he should "let go and let God" help him recover, which he believed would happen as long as he remained attuned to God. He said he believed God had a plan for his life, which he found comforting. He said that in his recent studies of the Bible he had been awestruck with how great and powerful God is and what a privilege it was to let this all-powerful being run his life.

Regarding religious activities, he said that he prayed frequently, particularly for relief from the "bondage" of his addiction. Prayer bolstered his confidence in his higher power's ability to help him remain abstinent, and this relieved some of his anxiety about the future. He said that attending worship services gave him an emotional lift, because they gave him hope for the future. Specifically, worship bolstered his faith "that God will help me not to drink, and that He will not abandon me even though I abandoned him." Similarly, reading the Bible gave him "joy" and "reassurance that I don't have to do it alone."

## Integrating the Twelve Steps into Clinical Work

With clients participating in twelve-step programs, the clinician should ask about what their higher power is and how it helps them to cope with urges and other problems. If clients have a religious orientation, the clinician can ask about how the twelve-step approach fits with their religious beliefs and practices. Where clients have mental health problems other than those addressed by their twelve-step groups, the clinician can ask if they also use the twelve steps and their higher power to cope with these problems.

## CLIENTS IN CRISIS: CRISIS AS DANGER AND OPPORTUNITY

The Chinese word for *crisis* can connote either "danger" or "opportunity." For centuries religion and mythology have emphasized that human growth and positive change can arise from crisis and trauma (Tedeschi, Park, and Calhoun, 1998). Joseph Campbell (1968) described how this theme is reflected in the three major stages common to world myths:

- The hero's call to adventure in an unfamiliar world
- The hero's encountering dangerous situations, emerging triumphant after an enormous struggle
- The hero's return to a familiar world with a transformed view of life

The myths of the world's great religions usually involve their heroes encountering a major crisis, the resolution of which leads them to key teachings. For example, Jesus faced the three temptations in the wilderness, the young Buddha discovered the aging of the body, and Moses had to lead the Israelites out of Egypt.

### Results of Empirical Studies

Empirical studies have examined whether meaning making is, in fact, associated with better long-term outcome after a crisis. Researchers have studied persons going through medical crises such as a heart attack and breast cancer, and through psychological crises such as divorce, bereavement, and disasters. They have found that a majority, or at least a large minority, of people do find benefits from a crisis or loss (Schaefer and Moos, 1998; Calhoun and Tedeschi, 2001), a process which can be termed "meaning making," "benefit finding," or "posttraumatic growth." On the other hand, a minority does not find benefit. Of these, some adjust well without finding meaning in a loss (Neimeyer, 2000). Some, however, "manifest long-term bitterness and suspiciousness" (Aldwin and Sutton, 1998, p. 57), or become locked into "ruminative thought" without finding meaning (Taylor et al., 2000, p. 105).

These studies have found that finding meaning after a crisis is associated with less emotional distress (Affleck and Tennen, 1996). Some evidence also suggests that, for those coping with an illness, finding meaning is associated with better physical outcomes (Taylor et al., 2000). For example, male heart attack victims who found meaning after the attack were less likely to have a subsequent attack (Affleck et al., 1987, cited in Taylor et al., 2000). Recently bereaved HIV-positive men who found meaning in the loss of their partners maintained higher levels of immunity over a two- to three-year period, whereas those who did not showed a decline in immunity and a higher mortality rate (Taylor et al., 2000).

One caution here is that most of these studies simply find an association between meaning making and better emotional and physical health. They do not prove that benefit finding caused the lower levels of distress. An alternative explanation is that those who adjust better to the crisis in the first place are more likely to find meaning in it.

## Types of Meaning Making Most Commonly Reported After Crisis

What types of meaning do people commonly find after a crisis? Here are several:

- Strengthening of relationships with family and friends (Affleck and Tennen, 1996).
- Increased empathy, compassion, and ability to connect emotionally with others (Affleck and Tennen, 1996; Tedeschi, Park, and Calhoun, 1998).
- Positive personality changes, including increased patience, tolerance, and courage (Affleck and Tennen, 1996). Despite an increased sense of vulnerability, many report being stronger people "simply because they have been able to go on" despite the loss (Calhoun and Tedeschi, 2001, p. 159).
- Changes in life's priorities and goals: People often ask the question, "What is really most important to me in life?" (Affleck and Tennen, 1996). For example, an HIV-positive man said:

> I feel . . . a strong sense that this is the only time we have, not next week, but now. Get everything you can out of living; do what you want to do, enjoy it. This feels like a positive thing, not a desperate thing—trying to treasure what's happening right now. (Schwartzberg, 1993, pp. 484-485)

- Facing mortality and greater acceptance of death (Tedeschi, Park, and Calhoun, 1998).
- Increased commitment to religion or spirituality (Tedeschi, Park, and Calhoun, 1998). Crisis often shatters people's optimistic assumptions about the world. This may trigger existential struggle and doubt, causing people to search for religious or spiritual answers (Calhoun and Tedeschi, 2001). Studies show that "a significant proportion of people who experience loss report that their spiritual or religious lives" have become more important and meaningful (Calhoun and Tedeschi, 2001, p. 161). They also show that religious people are more likely to report posttraumatic growth than nonreligious people. However, these studies have not sorted out a "chicken-and-egg" question: Does religion cause posttraumatic growth, or do people in crisis seek

out religion or increase their devotion to it (Calhoun et al., 2000)?

## Applications to Psychotherapy

For clients coping with trauma and loss, a primary task of the clinician is to help them rebuild "the damaged or shattered worldview," so that they can "develop a new life narrative that incorporates the loss in a helpful way" (Calhoun and Tedeschi, 2001, p. 166). Of course, it may take quite some time for the clinician to help the client do this. In the immediate aftermath of a crisis or loss, the therapist initially needs to focus on helping the client to minimize distress and cope with intrusive memories and thoughts (Janoff-Bulman and Frantz, 1997). However, as therapy continues, the clinician can listen for and facilitate the client's attempts to find meaning. Of course, the client's initial, provisional sense of meaning may change over time, so therapists need to listen for revisions (Neimeyer, 2000). Finally, a caution is in order: Therapists should not pressure clients to find meaning if they are not looking for it, because some people adjust well to crises without searching for meaning (Neimeyer, 2000). Also, pressuring clients to find meaning can be counterproductive because they may arrive at a sense of meaning that is artificial and premature.

## Case Example

Earlier in this book I emphasized the importance of doing a spiritual assessment at the time of the first or second interview. However, clients in crisis may be so overwhelmed by their distress that they cannot draw on their spiritual resources. Consequently, early in therapy they may minimize the importance of their religious beliefs and practices. However, later on, as the crisis subsides, they may draw on their faith to bring them out of the crisis, to find meaning in it, and to find hope for the future. This case illustrates such a pattern.

I saw an elderly man for psychotherapy to address his depression related to a life crisis involving a severe medical problem. He and his physician were alarmed that he had been experiencing insomnia and a severe loss of appetite and weight. His doctor was uncertain of the client's precise medical diagnosis and how much of his depression, insomnia, and anorexia were caused by his medical problem.

When I first saw him for therapy, he was expending all his effort just to get through each day. He often had to push himself to eat more food, to get more rest, and to exercise moderately. When I asked him about spiritual resources at the first session, he acknowledged that he had Christian beliefs and practices, but that he was not using them to cope with his current problem. Instead, he was consumed with worry about his medical problems, was completely puzzled about his loss of appetite, and was obsessed with maintaining as much of his health as he could. In the midst of this crisis, he focused strictly on keeping his "head above water."

As several weeks of diagnostic workups and treatment went by, his medical condition improved, as did his mood. At about the time of the tenth therapy session, I found him reading his Bible as he was waiting to see me. Surprised, I asked him about this. He said that he was elated by his medical progress, his restored appetite and sleep, and his recovery from depression. He had now returned to reading his Bible and praying on a daily basis. In the process he had received supportive "messages" from God, which assured him that God would support him in his continued physical and emotional recovery. His renewed spiritual practice bolstered his confidence in his ability to cope and to get his life back to normal.

## DEVOUTLY RELIGIOUS CLIENTS: RELIGIOUSLY ADAPTED THERAPY

Thus far, I have talked only about a broad-based ecumenical approach to intervention, one that can be adapted to the beliefs and practices of a wide range of religious clients. Another type of therapy, however, can be used when both the clinician and client share the same religious framework: religiously adapted psychotherapy. Here, the clinician may feel free to use common religious beliefs and language to intervene because he or she has thorough knowledge of the client's belief system.

Research shows that many devoutly religious clients prefer a therapist with similar orientation. As Worthington and colleagues (1996) state: "Highly religious Jews, Mormons, Protestants, and Roman Catholics usually prefer counseling with religiously similar counselors" (p. 459). However, even though they prefer having this common ground, they "do not want counselors to focus centrally on religion" (Worthington et al., 1996, p. 459). This preference for a religiously similar therapist underscores the importance of assessing clients' spirituality at the first session, so that the clinician can explore the possibility of such a preference and any fears clients may have in working with a clinician who does not share their belief system.

What are the components of religiously adapted therapy? Basically, they involve using religious beliefs and practices to augment psychotherapeutic strategies. Koenig and Pritchett (1998) note the following examples:

- "Listening to and validating healthy forms of religious coping" (p. 329)
- "Pointing out religious scriptures that provide hope, a positive self-esteem, and a sense that they are loved and cared for" (pp. 329-330)
- "Use of the patient's religious worldview to alter maladaptive, dysfunctional cognitions and encourage healthy behaviors" (p. 330)

For example, in the Christian tradition, a therapist could support clients' using meditation or prayer to cope; could cite teachings about grace and forgiveness to address unwarranted guilt; or could encourage clients to consider using resources within their churches, such as support groups or consultation with the minister.

Rational-emotive and cognitive-behavioral therapies are two types for which religiously adapted versions have been developed (Worthington et al., 1996). For example, Ellis (2000) notes that therapists from Protestant, Jewish, and Muslim religions have developed religiously adapted versions of rational self-statements for their clients. These rational statements are designed to address the irrational beliefs that Ellis, the founder of rational-emotive therapy, believes are the root of much emotional distress. For example, with regard to unconditional self-acceptance (USA), the secular version of the rational statement would be: "I can always choose to give myself USA and see myself as a 'good person' just because I am alive and human— whether or not I act well and whether or not I am lovable" (Ellis, 2000, p. 32). The "God-oriented" version of this would be:

> My God is merciful and will always accept me as a sinner while urging me to go and sin no more. Because God accepts the sinner, though not his or her sins, I can accept myself no matter how badly I behave. (Ellis, 2000, p. 32)

How effective is religiously adapted cognitive therapy for depression? In their review of empirical studies examining its efficacy with depressed clients, Worthington and colleagues (1996) conclude:

"Overall, religiously adapted cognitive therapy has been found to be effective with religious clients having mild depression but only marginally more effective than nonreligious versions" (p. 477).

## CONCLUSION

I have now described ways of assessing spirituality and using spiritually attuned methods of intervention. These may be used in the context of individual or group therapy and for psychoeducational purposes. Such therapy is the topic of the final chapter, which presents the psychoeducational spirituality group.

# Chapter 7

# The Psychoeducational Spirituality Group

The psychoeducational spirituality group is a six-session ecumenical class for mental health patients, church members, or any other group of people who are interested in how spirituality can enhance their mental health. In the spirit of this book's client-centered approach, its primary purpose is to help participants discover how their own spiritual beliefs and practices can enhance their emotional health.

## BACKGROUND

I originally created this class for use with VA outpatient substance abusers in early recovery. More recently, I used it with a group of dual-disorder patients in VA residential treatment and with a group of congregants at my church.

The psychiatric patients valued the class very much, sometimes to the point of wanting the class not to end. Staff also reacted positively to the class, because it complemented rather than duplicated other psychoeducational classes that were offered in the program. Staff commented that patients were talking in my group about issues that they had never brought up in their general psychotherapeutic groups. Furthermore, because many of the patients were recovering from substance abuse, the class fit very well with the spiritual approach that many of them were using in their twelve-step programs.

Why did patients talk in my group about major emotional issues that they ignored in other groups or classes? I think there are at least three reasons. First, unlike group therapy, the format was that of a structured class with assigned topics for each session, which forced them to examine each one. By contrast, in a therapy group patients could avoid or overlook certain painful topics, especially if others did not initiate talking about a particular problem area. The issues covered in my group included painful ones, such as unresolved grief, anger about past offenses, or guilt about their own misdeeds. Second, in other educational classes and therapy groups, spirituality was not explicitly invited into the discussion. Inviting patients to discuss their spiritual perspective on these issues can make for a more powerful and broad-based exploration. Third, the emphasis in many other classes was on "how to cope" with difficult emotions and to reduce them. In the psychoeducational spirituality class, this question was also addressed. However, the leaders also acknowledged the limits of our ability to change our circumstances and emotional states, which opened the door to clients' using spirituality to accept what they cannot change.

## *FACILITATORS*

On some occasions I led the group by myself, and on others I co-led it with a chaplain or an advanced trainee in the mental health field. I have found it better to have a coleader for three reasons. First, the coleader can offer complementary perspectives to my own. Second, I have someone who can run the class in the event that I cannot do so. If a class needs to be cancelled, the course often loses its momentum. Third, a second person listening to the content of the discussion and observing the group process is always helpful.

When two leaders are used, it is important to discuss how you will divide leadership responsibilities for the group. For example, will you share the brief lecture portion of each class or alternate the lecturer from session to session? How will you decide together during the group about any adaptations or changes in sequence that may be needed? For example, if the group seems particularly engaged in one discussion question or issue, you might together decide to forego other material to focus on that. I often prefer to make the observation aloud to the group (e.g., "This seems to be of great interest to you all") and then raise the question of what to do (e.g., "Shall we spend more time on this or move on?") with both my cofacilitator and the group. If cofacilitators sit across from each other in the group, rather than side by side, they can easily communicate verbally and non-verbally about these issues.

## Ministers As Cofacilitators in Mental Health Settings

For a class of mental health clients in which one coleader is a chaplain or minister, a number of issues need to be considered. If you have a choice of ministers or chaplains, you need to consider one who will be a good fit for the patients' religious backgrounds. If most of the patients tend to come from one religious perspective, having a chaplain from that background is preferable in case participants ask for clarification about the teachings of their religion. A minister from that background can help explain various points of view related to that issue. Another consideration in choosing a minister is whether that person has had some experience with mental health clients and understands something about their issues. Perhaps the most important quality is the chaplain's ability to take an accepting, nonjudgmental approach to the patients.

Obviously, this accepting approach also needs to encompass the patients' religious beliefs, especially because the group is ecumenical in spirit. Fortunately, at the Veterans Affairs medical center where I work, chaplains are required to take an approach that honors all faith traditions. In coleading this group with chaplains at the VA, I have found that they are very accepting of all traditions expressed in the group. If a minister is coleading the group, you should inform participants of this in advance, so that they can voice any concerns.

For a mental health professional, a major advantage of a cofacilitating minister is that the minister can address most questions related to religious beliefs and practices. This can be important because of the matters that I discussed in Chapter 3 on ethical issues. In particular, I do not want to address questions that are beyond my competence and training. If I am leading this group by myself and questions about belief and practice arise, I usually redirect clients to their minister or simply note that they are struggling with an issue. I do not try to answer the question, unless it is a more general, ecumenical question that is addressed by many different religions. I might then provide my sense of how different spiritual traditions would address it. When a minister is coleading the group and shares the religious tradition of those asking the religious questions, the minister then can provide his or her own answer to the questions.

### *Case Example*

I was coleading Session One with a Protestant chaplain for a group of patients, most of whom had dual disorders and most of whom identified themselves as Christian or Catholic. A few of the group members with addictions had experienced multiple relapses on substances during their lifetimes. They began to debate whether, once a person has failed a certain number of times, "God gives up on me" or "abandons me." I reflected back to the group that there seemed to be disagreement about this issue. Then, I turned to the chaplain to see if he wished to offer a viewpoint. He then gave his view of the issue, which he presented as his personal view and not as the "the one true answer." He said that he believed that God never chooses to abandon us, but if we choose to stop relating to God, then God's help is less available to us. We may choose to disconnect ourselves from God, but God does not do the same to us. The patients appreciated hearing his answer, whether or not they necessarily agreed, and the discussion moved on.

*Comment:* If I had been leading the group alone, I would have simply reflected the group's disagreement about the issue. One reason is that I personally do not have an opinion on the issue and do not know the various ways that Judeo-Christian religions would answer the question. The advantage of having a chaplain present is that he or she can comment on theological questions like this, ones that I do not wish or have the knowledge to comment on.

## *OVERVIEW OF THE SESSIONS*

A detailed facilitator's guide for the psychoeducational spirituality group is provided in Appendix A. Each one- to two-hour session is described in detail there. Here, I provide a very brief synopsis of each session. Note that the six sessions could be expanded into at least eight sessions by dividing the sessions on forgiveness and crisis into two different classes, as described in this chapter and in Appendix A. Regarding the order of the classes, session one should be the first one, but you could reorder the other five classes if you wish.

### *Session One: "What Is Spirituality for You?"*

So that the facilitators get a feel for the religious orientation and practices of group members, the Religious Background and Behaviors Scale is administered. Group discussion in this section focuses on questions concerning what spirituality is for each of them; what their concept of the sacred is, if any; what spiritual practices they use; and how their spiritual beliefs and practices help or hinder their coping with their problems.

## Session Two: Meditation Without Prescribed Religious Content

Group members are asked about their past and current experience with meditation. They are introduced to two major types of meditation: centering and mindfulness meditation, and then they participate in two meditation practice sessions lasting five to ten minutes each, with feedback after each about their experiences. They are not given any religious themes or images to incorporate into their meditation, but religious members are given permission to do so on their own if they want. They are told about the applications of meditation to coping with emotional distress and urges to use substances (e.g., urge surfing and mood surfing).

## Session Three: Coping with Grief

Participants take a few minutes of silence to reflect on loved ones who have passed on and who are currently dying. They are then invited to discuss their feelings about their bereavement and how they coped with or are coping with their grief. They are encouraged to include their religious perspectives on death and how those perspectives help (or hinder) their coping with grief.

## Session Four: Letting Go of Anger and Practicing Forgiveness

The presenters provide an overview of "letting go of anger" or "practicing forgiveness," emphasizing that the participants can choose whichever term is most helpful to them. Selected content from this topic in Chapter 5 is summarized, and participants discuss their views of these issues, including their religious perspectives on this issue. Then, participants take a few minutes of silence to reflect on (1) offenses that still trigger resentment or anger and (2) offenses that they previously resented but have since "let go" and how they did so. Alternatively, they may focus on similar questions regarding self-forgiveness. They are then invited to share the offenses that came to mind. For offenses that they have not forgiven, they are asked to describe where they currently stand on the issue: Do they wish to "let go of" some of this anger or not, and why? Another option is to divide this session into two parts: the first focusing on forgiving others and the second dealing with self-forgiveness.

### Session Five: Crisis As Danger and Opportunity

The leaders briefly summarize material from this section in Chapter 6, emphasizing that this is a major theme among world religions. Participants take a few minutes of silence to reflect on crises that they have weathered and whether they have experienced any growth from them.

Because crisis can change our fundamental values, the second part of this session focuses on the values survey (Chapter 2). After completing the survey, they are invited to summarize their top five values, to say why these values are important to them, and to state whether they believe they are living in accord with them. Facilitators may opt to make this second part on values a separate, additional session.

### Session Six: Gratitude

I have included a session on gratitude for three reasons. First, after dealing with emotionally difficult topics in sessions three, four, and five, the topic of gratitude is a positive way to end the course. Second, major world religions emphasize the importance of practicing gratitude (Carmen and Streng, 1989, cited in Emmons and McCullough, 2003). A recent study showed that people with a grateful disposition score higher on religiosity and "on nonsectarian measures of spirituality that assess spiritual experiences (e.g., sense of contact with the divine) and sentiments (e.g., belief that all living things are interconnected) independent of specific theological orientation" (McCullough, Emmons, and Tsang, 2002, p. 124). Third, recent research on gratitude has shown that a grateful disposition is associated with positive emotions. Specifically, McCullough, Emmons, and Tsang (2002) found that a grateful disposition, defined as a "generalized tendency to recognize and respond with grateful emotion" to others' benevolence, is associated with more positive emotions and fewer negative ones; with greater life satisfaction; and with more prosocial behavior, such as providing help and support (p. 112). More important, one series of studies showed that practicing gratitude appears to create better mood. In these studies Emmons and McCullough (2003) tested the effect of a daily or weekly gratitude intervention, in which people were asked to write down "up to five things in your life that you are grateful or thankful for" (p. 379). As compared with control interventions, the gratitude intervention created more positive emotions, and in one of the studies involving medical patients, it also reduced negative emotions (Emmons and McCullough, 2003). A caution here is that this research is only in the beginning stages. For a detailed review of theory and research related to the psychology of gratitude, see Emmons and McCullough (2004).

Unfortunately, I do not know of studies that have used a gratitude intervention with a group of mental health clients. Such studies would be helpful in providing guidelines for using it in the psychoeducational group.

In the meantime, I have used a gratitude exercise similar to that in the previously mentioned study. Participants are asked to look back over the past week and the past year and to make lists of things they are grateful for. The leader then asks them to share their lists. Finally, the leader asks them to reflect on discussion questions about gratitude.

## CONCLUSION

I consider this psychoeducational group to be a work in progress. My intention in each session is to provide a structured catalyst for group dialogue. Hopefully, this group discussion will make clear how the participants use their spirituality to cope and will provide them with additional spiritually related coping strategies. However, there is nothing magical about the way that I have structured the sessions. You should feel free to use this as a starting point and then to experiment and innovate from there, depending on your participants' needs.

# Appendix A

# The Psychoeducational Spirituality Group: A Guide for Group Facilitators

Prior to reading this appendix, please read Chapter 7 of this book, which provides an overview of the psychoeducational spirituality group. The six sessions of the group are as follows:

- Session One: "What Is Spirituality for You?"
- Session Two: Meditation Without Prescribed Religious Content
- Session Three: Coping with Grief
- Session Four: Letting Go of Anger and Practicing Forgiveness
- Session Five: Crisis As Danger and Opportunity
- Session Six: Gratitude

Instructions are provided next for running each session. These are simply loose guidelines and facilitators should adapt them according to the needs and abilities of their clients. Although I note an option for an additional session for topics four and five, you could hold multiple sessions for any of the topics.

## PLANNING: MATERIALS AND SESSION LENGTH

I use the following materials: grease board or flipchart, optional video player and monitor, and meditation bell for ending periods of silence. I do not usually give patients handouts, but I do for members of my church taking this as an adult education class. You may also wish to have a table in the middle of the group with an ecumenical sacred symbol, a candle, or other object suggesting the sacred.

Sessions can be one to two hours in length, depending on how many people are in your group and how much discussion you think they will engage in. The more people you have and the more insightful they are, the longer the time you will want to allow. I have found that for mental health groups of seven or eight patients, ninety-minute sessions have been a good length. However, for a group of ten to thirteen members of my church, two hours was better.

The figures and tables used in these sessions are contained in Appendix B. You can photocopy and use the forms as handouts, because The Haworth Press has granted permission for such.

## SESSION ONE: "WHAT IS SPIRITUALITY FOR YOU?"

### Introduction of Course

*The Religious Background and Behaviors Scale*

When participants arrive at class, they immediately fill out a Religious Background and Behaviors Questionnaire (see Appendix B) and return it to the facilitator, who then will glance over them to get a sense of the religious orientation and practices of group members. (Alternatively, this scale can be given to participants ahead of the class when they are being individually screened or oriented to it.) One of the facilitators should collate the responses to the first question (religious orientation) as the other is introducing the class, so that later he or she can describe to the group the religious distribution of the class.

*Introduction of Facilitator and Participants*

Introduce yourself. Then ask participants to introduce themselves and to say what they would like to gain from the course.

*Overview of the Course*

Describe what will be covered at each of the six sessions. Unless you have group members who share one faith tradition, emphasize that this class is conducted in an ecumenical spirit, in which all faith perspectives are respected and welcomed. You as the leader should briefly share your own religious or spiritual orientation with the group, so that they know this from the beginning. (Note: Later in this session you are providing your own definition of spirituality, but here you provide only a general statement about your orientation, e.g.: "I am a liberal Presbyterian and I believe important truths can be found in other religious faiths.")

*Format for Beginning and Ending Each Session*

Cover the following issues:

- Will you begin with a brief, one-minute check-in from each person? If so, tell the group or discuss with them the option of checking in.
- Will you be taking a break in the middle of each session?
- Decide if you wish to end each group session in a special way. For example, sometimes I have used an ecumenical prayer such as the Serenity Prayer. Other options would include a minute of silence or a very brief inspirational statement that is ecumenical in spirit.

*Open/Closed Group*

Let them know if the group is open to new members or whether it is closed to new people as of the first session. (If the group is constantly open to new members, then I recommend orienting new members to the group prior to their first session. They should be informed about the sessions they have missed and what the topic is for the session they are entering. You should give them the Religious Background and Behaviors Questionnaire, so you know a little about them. You can invite them to share their spiritual approach very briefly with the group at their first meeting if they wish.)

*Confidentiality*

If you are educating a group of mental health clients, ask the group members to agree to confidentiality. If you are conducting the group in a church or other non–mental health setting, I still recommend that the group agree to confidentiality. However, some leaders may wish to have the group discuss various options for confidentiality, such as strict confidentiality, confidentiality of what is shared only if the discloser requests it after sharing a particular comment, or permission to share what was said provided the name of the discloser is not mentioned.

*Ground Rules for Discussion*

Tell them the following:

- The emphasis is on respectful listening and tolerance of different points of view. Participants should not try to refute or challenge others' beliefs or practices.
- After the first session, participants do not need to bring spirituality and religion into the discussion if they do not want to do so. However,

their religious or spiritual perspectives on any issue is always welcome.

### Reflection, Lecture, and Discussion

#### "What Is Spirituality?"

Ask each participant to reflect on the question of what spirituality is for him or her. This can be done in many ways, but I have described two options here:

*Option one.* You can have participants become aware of their thoughts, feelings, and memories related to spirituality. In this way you can help them to be aware of the positive and negative sentiment about spirituality that they bring to the group. Some people attending may have had very painful experiences related to religion; they and the leader need to be aware of this. For others, spirituality has been the source of their most powerful life experiences. One way to enhance their awareness in this area is to have them pause for two minutes of silence to consider the following question: "When someone mentions spirituality or religion to you, what thoughts, feelings, or memories come to mind?" You can then invite them to briefly discuss these with the group. Even if they do not share their responses, they hopefully will have become more aware of their experiences of religion/spirituality.

*Option two.* A more experiential approach is to introduce this question with a brief section from a story, poem, or movie that has several spiritual dimensions. Tell them that, after reading it or showing it, you will give them two minutes of silent reflection after the segment to reflect on the following question: "What spiritual themes or feelings emerged for you, if any, from this reading/segment?" Then, ask for their responses and acknowledge their ideas.

#### Feedback About the Group's Religious Orientations

Note the distribution of religious orientation in the group, based on their responses to the Religious Background and Behaviors Questionnaire. Then inform the group about the distribution of participants' religious orientation, e.g., "Three of you identify yourselves as religious, four as spiritual, one as unsure, two as atheist, and three as agnostic." If this kind of diversity exists in the group, you can note it and proceed to the discussion questions. You should emphasize that you are interested in hearing not just from those who identify themselves as spiritual or religious, but from the others too, e.g., "Those of you who are agnostic or atheist may have some ideas about spirituality that you wish to share, and we are just as interested in hearing from you."

*Discussion Questions*

You can now introduce the discussion questions (see Exhibit A.1), which can be listed on a board or in a handout. Then ask the members to take a moment of silence to reflect on these questions. Tell them that they have the option of sharing their responses with the group, and that they do not need to respond to all the questions if they do not want to. Although the questions can be taken one at a time, I prefer to have participants respond to all the questions at once as they take turns. Usually each person can summarize his or her answers in about five minutes. Once a participant has shared his or her views, others may give feedback or ask questions.

*Suggestions for the Discussion*

Some of the discussion questions are personal in nature. If you are leading a group of church members who do not know one another very well, they may hesitate to share such personal information at the first session. To facilitate self-disclosure, the leaders may need to make it safer to share. One way to do this is to break up the group into dyads or triads for sharing their answers and then to reconvene the entire group to share any major insights that emerged.

---

### EXHIBIT A.1. Discussion Questions for Session One

1. If someone asked what spirituality is for you, what would you say?

2. Do you believe in a sacred being or supreme reality? If so, what do you call it?

3. What is your favorite spiritual practice (if any), and why? Do you find that some spiritual/religious practices create positive emotions or "highs" for you? If so, which practices do so and why? (Note that spiritual "practices" can include a wide variety of activities such as worship, meditation, prayer, attending church support groups, and visiting church members.)

4. Given the current problems in your life, how do your spiritual beliefs and practices help you cope with them? Are there any ways in which they have made your problems worse?

5. If you practice the twelve-step tradition, what do you consider your higher power?

Some people who are nonreligious find these questions difficult, and they may hesitate to answer. In these cases, acknowledge how difficult the questions can be, but emphasize that you want to start this workshop with the participants' views.

A few participants may tend to get bogged down in abstract philosophical or theological summaries of what they believe. When this happens, the leader must tactfully redirect the person(s) to discuss spirituality from a brief, more personal perspective. For example, if someone starts giving a long philosophical description of God, you could ask, "It sounds as if you've done quite a bit of thinking about God. How does that understanding of God help you relate to God?" The leader should not allow anyone to take a long time to answer the discussion questions; otherwise, some participants will have very little time.

If participants get into theological or philosophical arguments, remind them that in this group respectful listening and acceptance of different opinions is emphasized. Opposing perspectives can enrich the exchange, provided that participants respect these differences. When different perspectives emerge, the leaders can model tolerance for differences by simply noting them without favoring one side or the other.

Sometimes most of the participants will favor one religious system over others. In these cases I usually like to end the group by emphasizing that in future sessions we want to hear equally from the minority with other perspectives.

### Optional Presentation of Facilitator's Definition of Spirituality

After they respond to the discussion questions, one option is to present your own view of what spirituality is, as I do. I described my own view in Chapter 1. In explaining this view to the group, I give my definitions of spirituality and religion. I then draw Figure 1.1, the Primary Colors of Spirituality, on a grease board and explain the figure. Often they have already touched on these dimensions of spirituality in their discussion, so it simply reinforces what has been said. Another option is to present your own view of spirituality prior to the discussion questions, so that they have your ideas to consider in responding. However, my preference is to have them first state their own views.

### Closing

In closing, remind them that next week's topic is meditation.

## SESSION TWO: MEDITATION
## WITHOUT PRESCRIBED RELIGIOUS CONTENT

Ask the group members if they have had any further reflections on the nature of their own spirituality since the last session. Also ask about their experience, positive and negative, with current or past practice of meditation.

### Introduction to Meditation

Describe three purposes of meditation:

- Meditation as a *relaxation* technique: Studies have shown that meditation can lower blood pressure; decrease sympathetic nervous system arousal; and decrease cortisol levels (studies cited by Barnes, Treiber, and Davis, 2001).
- Meditation as a way of developing *"mindfulness,"* which is "to be aware of the full range of experiences that exist in the here and now" (Marlatt and Kristeller, 1999, p. 68). It is designed to enhance development of an *"observing self"* that watches one's thoughts and feelings as they occur, like clouds in the sky floating by.
- *Spiritual benefit:* Meditation may cultivate the "sense of inner calm, harmony and transcendence often associated with spiritual growth" by bypassing our usual daily preoccupations (Marlatt and Kristeller, 1999, p. 74).

Describe two types of meditation (Marlatt and Kristeller, 1999):

- *Concentrative meditation:* meditator focuses on a "specific object of attention, such as awareness of the breath" (p. 70).
- *Mindfulness meditation:* meditator focuses on any mental content as it occurs, including thoughts, feelings, and images.

Many other types of meditation exist, such as Transcendental Meditation and Christian meditation, and each religious tradition has its particular types. Sometimes meditation in these traditions involves repeating a religious term or phrase over and over (e.g., "om," "maranatha"). Tell the participants that, since this is an ecumenical group, they will practice only meditation without religious content. However, they are invited to add their own religious content or style to the meditation in their own individual practices. Tell them that another reason for practicing these two types of meditation is that they have direct applications to coping with stress. You may also add any other material that you wish from Chapter 4.

### Practice Sessions

Conduct two practice sessions each lasting five minutes or longer, with a discussion after each. The first session involves practicing concentrative meditation and the second uses mindfulness meditation. Use the instructions for the meditation shown in Chapter 4, Exhibit 4.1. After each session, invite the members to discuss how they experienced the meditation, as well as their success or frustration with it.

### Applications to Coping

After the mindfulness meditation and the ensuing discussion, you can describe a key application of mindfulness meditation to coping with stress: namely, developing an "observing self" that helps us to avoid "over-identifying" with our negative thoughts and feelings (Teasdale et al., 2002). This observing self can help us to step back from thoughts and feelings, observing them as a spectator, as we would clouds floating by in the sky. In mindfulness meditation we watch our thoughts, feelings, and images come and go. So too, in coping with emotional distress or urges to use substances, we can accept "what is" and let it pass. We can watch urges and negative moods come, and then watch them go.

One therapist has used the analogy of "surfing" (Marlatt and Kristeller, 1999):

- *Urge surfing* for substance abuse urges and other impulse control problems. A person carefully observes urges to use, identifies them as "just feelings" or "just thoughts," and refuses to see them as compulsions to relapse. Rather than seeing the urge to drink or use drugs as a giant tidal wave that will force the person into relapse, he or she sees it as just another wave that will come and go. In this way the person can "surf the urge" by watching it come and watching it go.
- *Mood surfing* for coping with emotional distress. Rather than seeing depression, anxiety, anger, or other unpleasant emotions as something one must immediately get rid of, a person can "surf the mood" by watching it come and watching it go.

Point out that they can also use active coping techniques, such as identifying and challenging negative thoughts, doing something pleasant, calling a friend or twelve-step sponsor, praying, doing a relaxation exercise, or taking medication. However, these coping methods often reduce the distress or urge only to a certain extent, leaving the person with some continuing discomfort. Sometimes the more the person fights the distress or urges, the worse the feelings get. For these reasons mindfulness can be a helpful additional coping strategy.

You may wish to contrast these two strategies by showing them the figure "Actively Reducing Distress versus 'Letting it Pass'" (see Appendix B). You can ask them for examples of the two strategies: "letting it pass" versus "actively reducing" distress. If necessary, you can supplement their answers with examples of your own. You can then emphasize that either strategy or a combination could be used at any given time. Finally, you can ask if anyone in the group has ever used this "letting it pass" method of coping with distress or urges to use substances, and what the experience was.

### Optional Third Meditation Session

If time remains, you may end this session with a third period of meditation, in which the members use whatever type they wish.

### Closing

Remind the class that meditation is a skill that, like any other skill, will improve with regular practice. Some people find it easier to practice with a group. You may wish to mention meditation groups that are available at your institution or community. Remind them that next week's topic is coping with grief.

## SESSION THREE: COPING WITH GRIEF

### Introduction

Ask if anyone had any further reflections on meditation or its applications since the most recent session.

### Silent Reflection

Remind them that today's topic is coping with grief. Give them instructions for reflection during a period of silence, as follows: "Take a few minutes of silence to reflect on loved ones who have passed on or loved ones who are currently dying. What feelings, thoughts, and memories come to mind?" Then give them two to three minutes of silence to reflect on this question.

One option in introducing this reflection is to use a reading or movie excerpt of a few minutes' duration, one that portrays death and dying with spiritual overtones. For example, you could read an excerpt from the book

*Tuesdays with Morrie,* or show an excerpt from the TV movie by the same name. Obviously, before reading the excerpt or showing the segment, provide the perspective of the entire story.

### Discussion

After the reflection, invite everyone to discuss the questions listed in Exhibit A.2. As before, I emphasize that they do not need to respond to all the questions, just those that they wish to.

### Closing

Remind the group of next week's topic, forgiveness.

### SESSION FOUR: LETTING GO OF ANGER
### AND PRACTICING FORGIVENESS

Ask if anyone has had any further reflections on grieving since the previous meeting.

### Introduction

Introduce today's topic as forgiveness. Note that many religions and the twelve-step tradition encourage the practice of forgiveness, which is why we include it in this group. Those who are not religious or feel uncomfort-

---

### EXHIBIT A.2. Discussion Questions for Coping with Grief

1.  Are you continuing to grieve for anyone you have lost in the past? If so, how do you express that continuing grief?

2.  Is there currently any friend or relative of yours who is dying now? How are you coping with that? What are your feelings about it?

3.  If you have a religious or spiritual perspective on death, you are welcome to share it with the group. Has this spiritual perspective on death helped you (or hindered you) in your efforts to cope with someone's death or dying?

4.  Has the loss of loved ones influenced your view of your own life and death? If so, how?

able with the term "forgiveness" may wish to use the term "letting go of anger." Tell them that if they have a spiritual or twelve-step perspective on forgiveness, they are welcome to bring that into today's discussion.

## Types of Forgiveness

Note the different types of forgiveness:

- Forgiving another with whom one no longer has a relationship
- Forgiving another with whom one still has an ongoing relationship
- Seeking forgiveness from another for one's own transgressions, as in the twelve-step tradition
- Self-forgiveness

You will need to decide if today's class will involve *only* offenses by another person or those of *both* others and oneself. If you decide to focus only on offenses by others in this session, you can hold an optional additional session on self-forgiveness; see the description of the optional session later in this section. Either way, tell them at this point whether both types of forgiveness will be discussed in this session.

## Definition and Overview of Forgiveness

Provide a general overview of your view of forgiveness and/or my view given in Chapter 5. If you use my material, I recommend including the following highlights:

- Mention one definition of forgiveness: "a significant decrease in negative thoughts and feelings toward a perceived transgressor, or, in the case of self-forgiveness, toward oneself." This definition does not require that one have a face-to-face reconciliation with the offender or "patching up" of the relationship, though that is always an option. You can then ask them for their own definitions of forgiveness, asking questions such as, "When you think of forgiveness, what do you picture?"
- Draw the "Continuum of Forgiveness" (see Appendix B) on a board. You could describe this as an "anger thermometer," with the hot end represented by "no forgiveness." Then write down their answers to the following questions about the various points on the continuum:
  —You should ask them for their ideas about the emotions and thoughts that are often associated with the "no forgiveness" end of the continuum (e.g., rage, resentment, constantly protesting that "it should never have happened").

—Concerning the "complete forgiveness" end of the continuum, you can point out that, by the definition of forgiveness given, complete forgiveness would involve no longer having negative emotional reactions when recalling the offense or offender. However, you can ask them for their definitions of "complete forgiveness," some of which may come from their religious traditions. Some may believe that such forgiveness involves developing positive feelings toward, reconciling with, or pardoning the offender.

—Finally, you can ask them to describe various gradations or phases of forgiveness that lie between the poles (e.g., no longer protesting that it occurred, ability to neutralize memories of the offense by distracting oneself, feeling only moderate anger when recalling it).

### Emphasize No Pressure to Forgive

Emphasize that in the class we do not pressure anyone to forgive. Rather, the intent is to invite participants to take an "inventory" of their offenses, in which they look at the price they are paying for holding on to anger about these. They can then consider the pros and cons of letting them go. Deciding not to forgive is acceptable. You could also ask them to describe some reasons that people may have for not wanting to forgive, as discussed in Chapter 5. For example, reconciling forgiveness with our demand that "justice be done" to the offender is difficult.

### How to Forgive

"How do I move toward letting go of anger or forgiveness?" Tell them that no consensus exists among professionals on "how to forgive." You can tell them that if they are already in psychotherapy or counseling, they can work with their therapist on this issue. If not, selected self-help books outline some of these theoretical "steps to forgiveness." Three are Luskin's *Forgive for Good* (2002), Spring's *How Can I Forgive You?* (2004), and Enright's *Forgiveness Is a Choice* (2001). If you wish, you can discuss some of the "theoretical phases of forgiveness" from Chapter 5. You can give examples of four techniques for letting go of anger that are described there.

- Gaining empathy for the offender, which may help one to understand why the person did it
- Challenging "unenforceable rules" about what others should or should not do to oneself

- Seeing the offender in the context of the "big picture" provided by one's religion or philosophy of life, e.g., "as God sees her," or "in cosmic perspective"
- Weighing how much blame the offender deserves for what happened; answering the question: "Am I taking complete responsibility for my contribution, if any, to what happened?"

### Silent Reflection

Now, tell the group members that you are going to invite them to take two minutes of silence to reflect on the following:

- Think of an offense from the past that angered you very much but which you have "let go of " or "forgiven," so that it no longer gets you very angry when you recall it.
- Think of an offense from the past that still gets you very angry when you recall it—one that you have not "let go of " or forgiven.

If you decided earlier to include in this session both forgiveness of others and oneself, remind them that they can focus on either kind in this exercise.

*Caution:* Some people may recall a particularly traumatic offense or event that evokes a painful reaction, especially flashbacks or other symptoms of post-traumatic stress disorder. If someone starts to talk about such an event, especially for the first time, the entire remaining time may be needed to support the person and suggest ways of coping with the memories. Thus, I recommend introducing the period of silent reflection in the following way:

> If any of you have experienced a very traumatic offense, such as a rape or assault, I ask that you not think about that during the silent reflection. Such memories could trigger strong feelings for you that you may need support in coping with. Because this is an educational group and not a therapy group, we are not able to provide the time you may need to discuss a traumatic offense. Please focus on less severe offenses that you have experienced. If you would like to discuss issues related to past trauma with a therapist, please see us afterward for a referral.

### Discussion

Then, have them discuss their answers to the questions in Exhibit A.3, if they are willing to share them.

## EXHIBIT A.3. Discussion Questions for Forgiveness

1.  Would you care to share an offense that you *have* let go of, and how you did so?

2.  Would you care to share an offense that you *have not* let go of? If so, would you say where you stand with regard to letting it go or not? If you do not wish to forgive this offense any more than you have, please say why. If you *do* wish to let go of more of your resentment, please say why, and ways that you would like to work toward forgiveness.

3.  If you have religious or spiritual beliefs about forgiveness, how do they influence your thoughts about forgiving or not forgiving offenses such as these?

### Closing

Remind them of next week's topic, "crisis as danger and opportunity." At the end of this session, you may wish to give participants the Values Survey (see Appendix B) to do as homework for Session 5, rather than taking five to ten minutes of the next session to have them do it.

## OPTIONAL ADDITIONAL SESSION ON SELF-FORGIVENESS

An additional session could focus on self-forgiveness rather than forgiving another person's offense. For brief lecture material, draw on the section on self-forgiveness in Chapter 5. Refer to the definition of self-forgiveness: "a decrease in negative thoughts and feelings toward oneself about a harmful mistake one has made." Refer also to the Continuum of Self-Forgiveness (see Appendix B). Ask them to describe the feelings and thoughts associated with the "no self-forgiveness" end of the continuum, those associated with "complete self-forgiveness," and those associated with points in between.

You then use a similar exercise of self-reflection. Tell them that you are going to invite them to take two minutes of silence to reflect on the following:

- Think of a mistake/misdeed that you regretted very much at the time, but which you have "let go of" or "forgiven" yourself for having done, so that it no longer gets you feeling very guilty when you recall it.
- Think of a mistake/misdeed that you committed in the past that still triggers lots of guilt when you recall it—one that you have not "let go of" or forgiven yourself for having done.

*Caution:* As in the session on forgiveness, some people may recall a particularly traumatic mistake or misdeed that evokes a great deal of painful emotion, especially strong guilt or flashbacks. If someone starts to talk about such an event, especially for the first time, too much time may be needed to support the person and suggest ways of coping with the memories.

Thus, I recommend introducing the silent reflection on self-forgiveness in the following way:

> If any of you have done something that brought severe harm to another person, such as having been the driver in an auto accident, you may feel free not to discuss it in detail in this group if you do not wish to, especially if you have not talked about it before with a therapist. Because this is an educational group and not a therapy group, we are not able to provide time for an in-depth hearing of each person's issues. I recommend that you focus on less severe mistakes or offenses that you have made in your life, ones that you can discuss briefly with the group after the silence. If you want to explore self-forgiveness for a difficult issue, I can talk with you afterward about referral to a therapist.

### Discussion

Then you can have them discuss their answers to the questions in Exhibit A.4.

### SESSION FIVE: CRISIS AS DANGER AND OPPORTUNITY

This session is composed of two parts but can be conducted as two separate sessions, particularly if you find that people want to talk more about their life crises in the first part. The first session would be titled Crisis as Danger and Opportunity. The second would be titled Values Clarification.

Ask if anyone has had any further reflections on "letting go of anger" or forgiveness since the previous meeting.

**EXHIBIT A.4. Discussion Questions for Self-Forgiveness**

1. Would you care to share a mistake/misdeed about which you no longer feel extremely guilty or self-critical, and how you arrived at that
   point?

2. Would you care to share a mistake/misdeed about which you still feel
   very guilty or self-critical? If you wish to move toward greater self-
   forgiveness, please say why, and ways that you have thought of for
   working on self-forgiveness. What are your thoughts about making
   amends or apologies to the one you offended, if that person is still
   available to you?

3. If you have religious or spiritual beliefs about self-forgiveness, how
   do they influence your thoughts about forgiving or not forgiving your
   own mistakes/misdeeds? Are there spiritual steps to self-forgiveness that you would consider?

## Values Survey

If you distributed the Values Survey (see Appendix B) the week before,
ask the members how many of them brought it with them this week. If some
did not, you will need to decide if you will just accept that those people will
not be able to participate during discussion of the survey. Alternatively, you
can reissue copies to those who do not have it and have them fill it out during a brief break taken right before the discussion of the survey.

## Part 1: Crisis As Danger and Opportunity

### Lecture

Introduce today's topic as Crisis As Danger and Opportunity. Note that
we experience many different types of life crises, some of which we have already covered in previous sessions. Some examples include

- losing a loved one or friend (bereavement),
- having someone offend us or betray us in a major way,
- suffering a major loss, e.g., job or possessions,
- major medical problems, and
- financial problems.

Summarize some of the content from Chapter 6's section titled Clients in Crisis: Crisis As Danger and Opportunity. I recommend sharing at least the following:

- Note that most religions and myths from around the world talk about life crisis as sowing the seeds of potential growth. Briefly summarize Joseph Campbell's stages of myth:
  —the hero's call to adventure,
  —the hero's encountering dangerous situations and then emerging triumphant after an enormous struggle, and
  —the hero's return to a familiar world with a transformed view of life.

You can invite them to cite examples of religious heroes who weathered a crisis and emerged with renewed strength, learning, or commitment.

- When people weather a crisis, finding meaning may help some people to cope with it better. Spirituality may be one resource for "making sense of" the crisis and finding strength to go on. However, finding meaning is not essential for coping well with a crisis: some people adapt well without finding meaning in it.
- Describe three examples of meaning making that people may engage in after a crisis:
  —Changes in life's priorities and goals: "What is really most important to me in life?"
  —Increased commitment to religion or spirituality may occur.
  —Positive personality changes, such as increased empathy and compassion for the suffering of others may give the person a stronger sense of connection with others.

## Emphasize Lack of Pressure to Find Meaning

Emphasize that you are not pressuring them to find meaning in a crisis if that has not emerged for them. Some people adjust well to a crisis without finding meaning in it, and it is counterproductive to force ourselves to find meaning prematurely.

## Silent Reflection

Have everyone do a two-minute period of silent reflection on the following questions: "During the past few years, what crises or major problems have you encountered? In the process of dealing with these crises, have you experienced any personal growth or important learning?"

*Caution:* Some people may recall a particularly traumatic event that evokes painful emotion. If someone starts to talk about such an event, especially for the first time, the entire remaining time may be needed to support the person and to suggest ways of coping with the memories. Thus, I recommend adding the following precaution:

> If any of you have had a very traumatic experience, such as a rape or combat experience, you may feel free not to discuss it in detail in this group if you do not wish to, especially if you have not talked about it before with a therapist. Because this is an educational group and not a therapy group, we are not able to provide time for an in-depth hearing of each person's crises. I recommend that you focus on less severe crises in your life that you can discuss briefly with the group after the silence.

### Discussion

Have them share their responses to the question for reflection. Emphasize that such sharing is optional.

### Preparation for Part 2

If you did not give them the Values Survey (Appendix B) from the week before, you now invite them to take five to ten minutes to fill it out. Go over the instructions with them and then have them complete the survey.

### Part 2: Values Survey

Remind the participants of the rationale for the Values Survey:

> In the process of finding meaning after a crisis, we may reprioritize our values in some important ways. That is why we are using the Values Survey. This survey also provides a way for you to take something concrete away from this course—a kind of road map for future reflection and action.

Have them answer the discussion questions from Exhibit A.5.

### Closing

Ask participants if they have any final comments or questions on today's topic.

## EXHIBIT A.5. Values Survey Discussion Questions

1. What are the values that you identified as your top five, and why?

2. Sometimes people list values that they are striving for, even though they recognize that they may not be fully living them out. To what extent are you living consistently with these values? If you are not satisfied with how consistently your actions match your values, are there ways you want to improve this fit?

3. Has a recent crisis, loss, or problem influenced any changes in these values in any way? In other words, do your current top values differ from those you would have marked in the recent past?

## SESSION SIX: GRATITUDE

### Introduction

Ask if anyone has any further reflections on last week's topics, "Crisis As Danger and Opportunity" and the "Values Survey."

### Overview of Gratitude

Tell them that today's topic is gratitude. Tell them that all of the world's religions and the twelve-step tradition emphasize the importance of gratitude. If you wish, briefly summarize some of the recent research on gratitude and its relationship with better mood, as described in the last part of Chapter 7. Another option is for a coleading minister or another coleader to summarize some spiritual or twelve-step teachings about the importance of gratitude, or to offer a reading on gratitude.

A caution here is that leaders must be careful not to discount the stress and crises that the participants are experiencing. We do not want clients to get the message: "Stop complaining and just focus on the positive." To guard against this, acknowledge that they are struggling to accept difficult losses and that consequently it may be difficult for them to feel grateful for anything. However, you should emphasize that in the midst of these losses, it is often easy to overlook our blessings. You then invite them to do the exercise, while also assuring them that it is acceptable if they decide there is nothing that they are grateful for at the present time.

*Exercise*

Hand out a piece of paper and pen to participants. Ask them to take a few minutes of silence to look back over the past week and the past year and to search for things that happened for which they are grateful. Ask them to make a list of at least five things they are grateful for: five from the past week and five from the past year.

*Discussion*

First, invite them to share their gratitude lists with the group if they wish. Next, ask them to reflect on discussion questions listed in Exhibit A.6.

Encourage them to continue practicing gratitude in the weeks ahead, perhaps by periodically repeating the exercise if they found it valuable.

**Closing**

Thank them for their participation in the spirituality group. Ask if they have any final questions or comments on the group as a whole.

---

### EXHIBIT A.6. Discussion Questions for Gratitude

1.  How important is practicing gratitude to you, and why?

2.  How do you practice it?

3.  If you practice gratitude, what benefits do you experience?

4.  What does your spiritual or religious orientation teach about gratitude?

# Appendix B

# Reproducible Material

On the following pages are tables and figures from the book that are used in the psychoeducational spirituality group. These have all appeared earlier in the book. Here, they are formatted for easy copying and have had the labels *exhibit, table,* or *figure* removed from their headings. These forms may be duplicated for your own use.

# THE RELIGIOUS BACKGROUND
# AND BEHAVIORS QUESTIONNAIRE

1. Which of the following best describes you at the present time? (Check one.)

_____ Atheist: I do not believe in a sacred being or supreme reality, such as God, Brahman, Allah, or nirvana.

_____ Agnostic: I believe we can't really know about a sacred being or supreme reality, such as God, Brahman, Allah, or nirvana.

_____ Unsure: I don't know what to believe about a sacred being or supreme reality, such as God, Brahman, Allah, or nirvana.

_____ Spiritual: I'm not religious, but I believe in a sacred being or supreme reality, such as God, Brahman, Allah, or nirvana.

_____ Religious: I practice religion and believe in a sacred being or supreme reality, such as God, Brahman, Allah, or nirvana.

2. For the *past year*, how often have you done the following? (Circle one number for each line.)

| | Never | Rarely | Once or twice a month | Once or twice a week | Almost daily | More than once a day |
|---|---|---|---|---|---|---|
| a. Thought about a sacred being or supreme reality | 1 | 2 | 3 | 4 | 5 | 6 |
| b. Prayed | 1 | 2 | 3 | 4 | 5 | 6 |
| c. Meditated | 1 | 2 | 3 | 4 | 5 | 6 |
| d. Attended religious services | 1 | 2 | 3 | 4 | 5 | 6 |
| e. Read scriptures or holy writings | 1 | 2 | 3 | 4 | 5 | 6 |
| f. Had direct experiences of a sacred being or supreme reality | 1 | 2 | 3 | 4 | 5 | 6 |

3. Have you *ever* in your life:

| | Never | Yes, in the past but not now | Yes, and I still do |
|---|---|---|---|
| a. Believed in a sacred being or supreme reality? | 1 | 2 | 3 |
| b. Prayed? | 1 | 2 | 3 |
| c. Meditated? | 1 | 2 | 3 |
| d. Attended religious services regularly? | 1 | 2 | 3 |
| e. Read or studied scriptures or holy writings regularly? | 1 | 2 | 3 |
| f. Had direct experiences of a sacred being or supreme reality? | 1 | 2 | 3 |

*Source:* Adapted from Center on Alcoholism, Substance Abuse and Addictions, 1994.

# VALUES SURVEY

The purpose of this exercise is to help you identify what you value most, so that you can set meaningful life goals and treatment goals.

Following is a list of eighty-three values. Please read through the list and identify the five values that are most important to you. Do this in two steps. First, as you read the values, place a check mark beside those that are very important to you. Then, looking over those checked, designate your top five values by numbering them 1 to 5, with 1 being the most important.

## List of Values

_____ Acceptance: to be accepted as I am

_____ Accuracy: to be correct in my opinions and actions

_____ Achievement: to accomplish and achieve

_____ Adventure: to have new and exciting experiences

_____ Attractiveness: to be physically attractive

_____ Authority: to be in charge of others

_____ Autonomy: to be self-determining and independent

_____ Beauty: to appreciate beauty around me

_____ Caring: to take care of others

_____ Challenge: to take on difficult tasks and problems

_____ Change: to have a life full of change and variety

_____ Comfort: to have a pleasant, enjoyable life

_____ Commitment: to make a long-lasting and deep commitment to another person

_____ Compassion: to feel and show concern for others

_____ Contribution: to make a contribution that will last after I am gone

_____ Cooperation: to work collaboratively with others

_____ Courtesy: to be polite and considerate to others

_____ Creativity: to have new and original ideas

_____ Dependability: to be reliable and trustworthy

_____ Duty: to carry out my duties and responsibilities

_____ Ecology: to live in harmony with and protect the environment

_____ Excitement: to have a life full of thrills and stimulation

_____ Faithfulness: to be loyal and reliable in relationships

_____ Fame: to be known and recognized

_____ Family: to have a loving, happy family

_____ Fitness: to be physically fit and strong

_____ Flexibility: to adjust to new or unusual situations easily

_____ Forgiveness: to be forgiving of others

_____ Friendship: to have close, supportive friends

_____ Fun: to play and have fun

_____ Generosity: to give what I have to others

_____ Genuineness: to behave in a manner that is true to who I am

_____ God's will: to seek and obey the will of God

_____ Growth: to keep changing and growing

_____ Health: to be physically well and healthy

_____ Helpfulness: to be helpful to others

_____ Honesty: to be truthful and genuine

_____ Hope: to maintain a positive and optimistic outlook

_____ Humility: to be modest and unassuming

_____ Humor: to see the humorous side of myself and the world

_____ Independence: to be free from depending on others

\_\_\_\_\_ Industry: to work hard and well at my life tasks

\_\_\_\_\_ Inner peace: to experience personal peace

\_\_\_\_\_ Intimacy: to share my innermost experience with others

\_\_\_\_\_ Justice: to promote equal and fair treatment for all

\_\_\_\_\_ Knowledge: to learn and possess valuable knowledge

\_\_\_\_\_ Leisure: to take time to relax and enjoy

\_\_\_\_\_ Loved: to be loved by those close to me

\_\_\_\_\_ Loving: to give love to others

\_\_\_\_\_ Mastery: to be competent in my everyday activities

\_\_\_\_\_ Mindfulness: to live conscious and mindful of the present moment

\_\_\_\_\_ Moderation: to avoid excesses and find a middle ground

\_\_\_\_\_ Monogamy: to have one close, loving relationship

\_\_\_\_\_ Nonconformity: to question and challenge authority and norms

\_\_\_\_\_ Nurturance: to take care of and nurture others

\_\_\_\_\_ Openness: to be open to new experiences, ideas, and options

\_\_\_\_\_ Order: to have a life that is well-ordered and organized

\_\_\_\_\_ Passion: to have deep feelings about ideas, activities, or people

\_\_\_\_\_ Pleasure: to feel good

\_\_\_\_\_ Popularity: to be well-liked by many people

\_\_\_\_\_ Power: to have control over others

\_\_\_\_\_ Purpose: to have meaning and direction in my life

\_\_\_\_\_ Rationality: to be guided by reason and logic

\_\_\_\_\_ Realism: to see and act realistically and practically

_____ Responsibility: to make and carry out important decisions

_____ Risk: to take risks and chances

_____ Romance: to have intense, exciting love in my life

_____ Safety: to be safe and secure

_____ Self-acceptance: to like myself as I am

_____ Self-control: to be self-disciplined and govern my own actions

_____ Self-esteem: to feel positive about myself

_____ Self-knowledge: to have a deep, honest understanding of myself

_____ Service: to be of service to others

_____ Sexuality: to have an active and satisfying sex life

_____ Simplicity: to live life simply, with minimal needs

_____ Solitude: to have time and space where I can be apart from others

_____ Spirituality: to grow and mature spiritually

_____ Stability: to have a life that stays fairly consistent

_____ Tolerance: to accept and respect those different from me

_____ Tradition: to follow respected patterns of the past

_____ Virtue: to live a morally pure and excellent life

_____ Wealth: to have plenty of money

_____ World peace: to work to promote peace in the world

*Source:* Adapted from Miller et al., 2001

"Letting it pass"
(mindfulness)                                                Actively reducing
                                                                distress

Actively Reducing Distress versus "Letting it Pass"

No forgiveness ⟷ Complete forgiveness

Continuum of Forgiveness

No
self-forgiveness

Complete
self-forgiveness

Continuum of Self-Forgiveness

# References

Affinito, M.G. (2002). Forgiveness in counseling: Caution, definition, and application. In S. Lamb and J.G. Murphy (Eds.), *Before forgiving: Cautionary views of forgiveness in psychotherapy* (pp. 88-111). New York: Oxford.

Affleck, G. and Tennen, H. (1996). Construing benefits from adversity: Adaptational significance and dispositional underpinnings. *Journal of Personality, 64,* 899-922.

Affleck, G., Tennen, H., Croog, S., and Levine, S. (1987). Causal attribution, perceived benefits, and morbidity after a heart attack: An eight-year study. *Journal of Consulting and Clinical Psychology, 55,* 29-35.

Alcoholics Anonymous (1976). *Alcoholics Anonymous* (Third edition). New York: Alcoholics Anonymous World Services.

Aldwin, C.M. and Sutton, K.J. (1998). A developmental perspective on posttraumatic growth. In R.G. Tedeschi, C.L. Park, and L.G. Calhoun (Eds.), *Posttraumatic growth: Positive changes in the aftermath of crisis* (pp. 43-64). Mahwah, NJ: Lawrence Erlbaum.

Almond, P.C. (1982). *Mystical experience and religious doctrine: An investigation of mysticism in world religions.* New York: Mouton Publishers.

American Psychiatric Association (1994). *Diagnostic and statistical manual of mental disorders* (Fourth edition). Washington, DC: American Psychiatric Association.

American Psychological Association (1993). Guidelines for providers of psychological services to ethnic, linguistic and culturally diverse populations. *American Psychologist, 48,* 45-48.

American Psychological Association (2002). Ethical principles of psychologists and code of conduct. *American Psychologist, 57,* 1060-1073.

American Psychological Association (2003). Guidelines on multicultural education, training, research, practice, and organizational change for psychologists. *American Psychologist, 58,* 377-402.

Applebaum, P.S., Robbins, P.C., and Roth, L.H. (1999). Dimensional approaches to delusions: Comparison across types and diagnoses. *American Journal of Psychiatry, 156,* 1938-1943.

Askin, H., Paultre, Y., White, R., and Van Ornum, W. (1993). The quantitative and qualitative aspects of scrupulosity. Paper presented at the annual convention of the American Psychological Association, Toronto. August 1993.

Atallah, S.F., El-Dosoky, A.R., Coker, E.M., Nabil, K.M., and El-Islam, M.F. (2001). A 22-year retrospective analysis of the changing frequency and patterns of religious symptoms among inpatients with psychotic illness in Egypt. *Social Psychiatry and Psychiatric Epidemiology, 36,* 407-415.

Baer, R.A. (2003). Mindfulness training as a clinical intervention: A conceptual and empirical review. *Clinical Psychology: Science and Practice, 10,* 125-143.

Barnes, V.A., Treiber, F.A., and Davis, H. (2001). Impact of Transcendental Meditation on cardiovascular function at rest and during acute stress in adolescents with high normal blood pressure. *Journal of Psychosomatic Research, 51,* 597-605.

Bentall, R.P. (1990). The illusion of reality: A review and integration of psychological research on hallucinations. *Psychological Bulletin, 107,* 82-95.

Bentall, R.P. (2000). Hallucinatory experiences. In E. Cardena, S.J. Lynn, and S. Krippner (Eds.), *Varieties of anomalous experience: Examining the scientific evidence* (pp. 85-120). Washington, DC: American Psychological Association.

Bishop, S.R. (2002). What do we really know about mindfulness-based stress reduction? *Psychosomatic Medicine, 64,* 71-84.

Bourguignon, E. (1970). Hallucinations and trance: An anthropologist's perspective. In W. Keup (Ed.), *Origins and mechanisms of hallucinations* (pp. 83-90). New York: Plenum.

Burnham, S. (1997). *The ecstatic journey: The transforming power of mystical experience.* New York: Ballantine Books.

Calhoun, L.G., Cann, A., Tedeschi, R.G., and McMillan, J. (2000). A correlational test of the relationship between posttraumatic growth, religion and cognitive processing. *Journal of Traumatic Stress, 13,* 521-527.

Calhoun, L.G. and Tedeschi, R.G. (2001). Posttraumatic growth: The positive lessons of loss. In R.A. Neimeyer (Ed.), *Meaning reconstruction and the experience of loss* (pp. 157-172). Washington, DC: American Psychological Association.

Campbell, J. (1968). *The hero with a thousand faces.* Princeton, NJ: Princeton University Press.

Cardena, E., Lynn, S.J., and Krippner, S. (Eds.) (2000). *Varieties of anomalous experience: Examining the scientific evidence.* Washington, DC: American Psychological Association.

Carman, J.B. and Streng, F.J. (Eds.) (1989). *Spoken and unspoken thanks: Some comparative soundings.* Dallas, TX: Center for World Thanksgiving.

Center on Alcoholism, Substance Abuse, and Addictions (CASAA) (1994). Religious practices and beliefs (RPB 21). University of New Mexico. Available online at <http://casaa.unm.edu>.

Chirban, J.T. (2001). Assessing religious and spiritual concerns in psychotherapy. In T.G. Plante and A.C. Sherman (Eds.), *Faith and health: Psychological perspectives* (pp. 265-290). New York: Guilford.

Connors, G.J., Toscova, R.T., and Tonigan, J.S. (1999). Serenity. In W.R. Miller (Ed.), *Integrating spirituality into treatment: Resources for practitioners* (pp. 235-250). Washington, DC: American Psychological Association.

Coyle, C.T. and Enright, R.D. (1997). Forgiveness intervention with postabortion men. *Journal of Consulting and Clinical Psychology, 65,* 1042-1046.

The Dalai Lama (1999). *Ethics for the new millennium.* New York: Riverhead Books.

Dass, Ram (1987). *Grist for the mill.* Berkeley, CA: Celestial Arts.

Dittrich, A., von Arx, S., and Staub, S. (1985). International study on altered states of consciousness: Summary of the results. *German Journal of Psychology, 9,* 319-339.

Eillis, A. (2000). Can rational emotive behavior therapy (REBT) be effectively used with people who have devout beliefs in God and religion? *Professional Psychology: Research and Practice, 31,* 29-33.

Ellison, C.G. and Levin, J.S. (1998). The religion-health connection: Evidence, theory, and future direction. *Health Education and Behavior, 25,* 700-720.

Emmons, R.A. and McCullough, M.E. (2003). Counting blessings versus burdens: An experimental investigation of gratitude and subjective well-being in daily life. *Journal of Personality and Social Psychology, 84,* 377-389.

Emmons, R.A. and McCullough, M.E. (Eds.) (2004). *The psychology of gratitude.* New York: Oxford University Press.

Enright, R.D. (2001). *Forgiveness is a choice.* Washington, DC: American Psychological Association.

Enright, R.D. and Fitzgibbons, R.P. (2000). *Helping clients forgive: An empirical guide for resolving anger and restoring hope.* Washington, DC: American Psychological Association.

Enright, R.D., Freedman, S., and Rique, J. (1998). The psychology of interpersonal forgiveness. In R.D. Enright and J. North (Eds.), *Exploring forgiveness* (pp. 46-62). Madison: University of Wisconsin Press.

Exline, J.J. and Baumeister, R.F. (2000). Expressing forgiveness and repentance: Benefits and barriers. In M.E. McCullough, K.I. Pargament, and C.E. Thoresen (Eds.), *Forgiveness: Theory, research, and practice* (pp. 133-155). New York: Guilford.

Finn, M. and Rubin, J.B. (2000). Psychotherapy with Buddhists. In P.S. Richards and A.E. Bergin (Eds.), *Handbook of psychotherapy and religious diversity* (pp. 317-340). Washington, DC: American Psychological Association.

Freedman, S.R. and Enright, R.D. (1996). Forgiveness as an intervention goal with incest survivors. *Journal of Consulting and Clinical Psychology, 64,* 983-992.

Gallagher, W. (1999). *Working on God.* New York: Random House.

Goldstein, J. and Kornfield, J. (1987). *Seeking the heart of wisdom: The path of insight meditation.* Boston: Shambhala.

Goleman, D. (2003). *Destructive emotions: A scientific dialogue with the Dalai Lama.* New York: Bantam Books.

Hanh, T.H. (1997). *Teachings on love.* Berkeley, CA: Parallax Press.

Horgan, J. (2003). *Rational mysticism: Dispatches from the border between science and spirituality.* New York: Houghton Mifflin.

James, W. ([1902] 1985). *The varieties of religious experience.* Cambridge, MA: Harvard University Press.

Janoff-Bulman, R. and Frantz, C.M. (1997). The impact of trauma on meaning: From meaningless world to meaningful life. In M. Power and C.R. Brewin (Eds.), *The transformation of meaning in psychological therapies: Integrating theory and practice* (pp. 91-106). New York: John Wiley.

Johns, L.C. and van Os, J. (2001). The continuity of psychotic experiences in the general population. *Clinical Psychology Review, 21,* 1125-1141.

Johnson, W.B., Ridley, C.R., and Nielsen, S.R. (2000). Religiously sensitive rational emotive behavior therapy: Elegant solutions and ethical risks. *Professional Psychology: Research and Practice, 31,* 14-20.

Kabat-Zinn, J. (2003). Mindfulness-based interventions in context: Past, present and future. *Clinical Psychology: Research and Practice, 10,* 144-156.

Koenig, H.G. and Pritchett, J. (1998). Religion and psychotherapy. In H.G. Koenig (Ed.), *Handbook of religion and mental health* (pp. 323-336). San Diego: Academic Press.

Krause, N. and Ingersoll-Dayton, B. (2001). Religion and the process of forgiveness in late life. *Review of Religious Research, 42(3),* 252-276.

Lamb, S. (2002). Women, abuse, and forgiveness: A special case. In S. Lamb and J.G. Murphy (Eds.), *Before forgiving: Cautionary views of forgiveness in psychotherapy* (pp. 155-171). New York: Oxford.

Lamb, S. and Murphy, J.G. (Eds.) (2002). *Before forgiving: Cautionary views of forgiveness in psychotherapy.* New York: Oxford.

Luskin, F. (2002). *Forgive for good.* New York: HarperCollins.

Malcolm, W.M. and Greenberg, L.S. (2000). Forgiveness as a process of change in individual psychotherapy. In M.E. McCullough, K.I. Pargament, and C.E. Thoresen (Eds.), *Forgiveness: Theory, research, and practice* (pp. 179-203). New York: Guilford.

Marlatt, G.A. and Kristeller, J.L. (1999). Mindfulness and meditation. In W.R. Miller (Ed.), *Integrating spirituality into treatment: Resources for practitioners* (pp. 67-84). Washington, DC: American Psychological Association.

McCullough, M.E., Emmons, R.A., and Tsang, J. (2002). The grateful disposition: A conceptual and empirical topography. *Journal of Personality and Social Psychology, 82,* 112-127.

McCullough, M.E., Pargament, K.I., and Thoresen, C.E. (2000). The psychology of forgiveness: History, conceptual issues, and overview. In M.E. McCullough, K.I. Pargament, and C.E. Thoresen (Eds.), *Forgiveness: Theory, research, and practice* (pp. 1-14). New York: Guilford.

Miller, W.R., C'deBaca, J., Matthews, D.B., and Wilbourne, P.L. (2001). Personal values card sort. University of New Mexico. Available online at the Center on Alcoholism, Substance Abuse, and Addictions, <http://casaa.unm.edu>.

Mora, G. (1969). The scrupulosity syndrome. In E.M. Pattison (Ed.), *Clinical psychiatry and religion* (pp. 163-174). Boston: Little, Brown.

Myers, D.G. (2000). The funds, friends, and faith of happy people. *American Psychologist, 55,* 56-67.

Neimeyer, R.A. (2000). Searching for the meaning of meaning: Grief therapy and the process of reconstruction. *Death Studies, 24,* 541-558.

Newberg, A.B. and d'Aquili, E.G. (1998). The neuropsychology of spiritual experience. In H.G. Koenig (Ed.), *Handbook of religion and mental health* (pp. 75-94). San Diego: Academic Press.

Otto, R. (1970). *The idea of the holy.* New York: Oxford University Press.

Pargament, K.I. (1992). Of means and ends: Religion and the search for significance. *The International Journal for the Psychology of Religion, 1,* 201-229.

Pargament, K.I. (1997). *The psychology of religion and coping: Theory, research, and practice.* New York: Guilford.

Pargament, K.I., McCullough, M.E., and Thoresen, C.E. (2000). The frontier of forgiveness: Seven directions for psychological study and practice. In M.E. McCullough, K.I. Pargament, and C.E. Thoresen (Eds.), *Forgiveness: Theory, research, and practice* (pp. 299-320). New York: Guilford.

Pargament, K.I., Zinnbauer, B.J., Scott, A.B., Butter, E.M., Zerowin, J., and Stanik, P. (1998). Red flags and religious coping: Identifying some religious warning signs among people in crisis. *Journal of Clinical Psychology, 54,* 77-89.

Plante, T.G. and Sherman, A.C. (2001). Research on faith and health. In T.G. Plante and A.C. Sherman (Eds.), *Faith and health: Psychological perspectives* (pp. 1-12). New York: Guilford.

Powell, L.H., Shahabi, L., and Thoresen, C.E. (2003). Religion and spirituality: Linkages to physical health. *American Psychologist, 58,* 36-52.

Richards, P.S. and Bergin, A.E. (1997). *A spiritual strategy for counseling and psychotherapy.* Washington, DC: American Psychological Association.

Richards, P.S., Rector, J.M., and Tjeltveit, A.C. (1999). Values, spirituality, and psychotherapy. In W.R. Miller (Ed.), *Integrating spirituality into treatment: Resources for practitioners* (pp. 133-160). Washington, DC: American Psychological Association.

Rye, M.S., Pargament, K.I., Ali, M.A., Beck, G.L., Dorff, E.N., Hallisey, C., Narayanan, V., and Williams, J.G. (2000). Religious perspectives on forgiveness. In M.E. McCullough, K.I. Pargament, and C.E. Thoresen (Eds.), *Forgiveness: Theory, research, and practice* (pp. 17-40). New York: Guilford.

Sanderson, C. and Linehan, M.M. (1999) Acceptance and forgiveness. In W.R. Miller (Ed.), *Integrating spirituality into treatment: Resources for practitioners* (pp. 199-216). Washington, DC: American Psychological Association.

Schaefer, J.A. and Moos, R.H. (1998). The context for posttraumatic growth: Life crises, individual and social resources, and coping. In R.G. Tedeschi, C.L. Park, and L.G. Calhoun (Eds.), *Posttraumatic growth: Positive changes in the aftermath of crisis* (pp. 99-125). Mahwah, NJ: Lawrence Erlbaum.

Schwartzberg, S.S. (1993). Struggling for meaning: How HIV-positive gay men make sense of AIDS. *Professional Psychology: Research and Practice, 24,* 483-490.

Segal, Z.V., Williams, J.M.G., and Teasdale, J.D. (2002). *Mindfulness-based cognitive therapy for depression.* New York: Guilford.

Smith, H. (1991). *The world's religions*. San Francisco: Harper.

Smith, T.B., McCullough, M.E., and Poll, J. (2003). Religiousness and depression: Evidence for a main effect and moderating influence of stressful life events. *Psychological Bulletin, 129,* 614-636.

Spilka, B., Hood, R.W., Hunsberger, B., and Gosuch, R. (2003). *The psychology of religion: An empirical approach.* New York: Guilford.

Spring, J.A. (2004). *How can I forgive you? The courage to forgive, the freedom not to.* New York: HarperCollins.

Stace, W.T. (1961). *Mysticism and philosophy.* London: Macmillan.

Taylor, S.E., Kemeny, M.E., Reed, G.M., Bower, J.E., and Gruenewald, T.L. (2000). Psychological resources, positive illusions, and health. *American Psychologist, 55,* 99-109.

Teasdale, J.D., Moore, R.G., Hayhurst, H., Pope, M., Williams, S., and Segal, Z.V. (2002). Metacognitive awareness and prevention of relapse in depression: Empirical evidence. *Journal of Consulting and Clinical Psychology, 70,* 275-287.

Tedeschi, R.G., Park, C.L., and Calhoun, L.G. (1998). Posttraumatic growth: Conceptual issues. In R.G. Tedeschi, C.L. Park, and L.G. Calhoun (Eds.), *Posttraumatic growth: Positive changes in the aftermath of crisis* (pp. 1-22). Mahwah, NJ: Lawrence Erlbaum.

Thoresen, C.E. (1999). Spirituality and health: Is there a relationship? *Journal of Health Psychology, 4,* 291-300.

Tien, A.Y. (1991). Distributions of hallucinations in the population. *Social Psychiatry and Psychiatric Epidemiology, 26,* 287-292.

Tonigan, J.S., Toscova, R.T., and Connors, G.J. (1999). Spirituality and the 12-step programs: A guide for clinicians. In W.R. Miller (Ed.), *Integrating spirituality into treatment: Resources for practitioners* (pp. 111-131). Washington, DC: American Psychological Association.

Warner, M. (1976). *Alone of all her sex: The myth and the cult of the Virgin Mary.* New York: Alfred Knopf.

Wiesenthal, S. (1976). *The sunflower: On the possibilities and limits of forgiveness.* New York: Schocken Books.

Winzelberg, A. and Humphreys, K. (1999). Should patients' religiosity influence clinicians' referral to 12-step self-help groups? Evidence from a study of 3,018 male substance abuse patients. *Journal of Consulting and Clinical Psychology, 67,* 790-794.

Worthington, E.L., Kurusu, T.A., McCullough, M.E., and Sandage, S.J. (1996). Empirical research on religion and psychotherapeutic processes and outcomes: A 10-year review and research prospectus. *Psychological Bulletin, 119,* 448-487.

Wulff, D.M. (2000). Mystical experience. In E. Cardena, S.J. Lynn, and S. Krippner (Eds.), *Varieties of anomalous experience: Examining the scientific evidence* (pp. 397-440). Washington, DC: American Psychological Association.

Zinnbauer, B.J., Pargament, K.I., Cole, B., Rye, M.S., Butter, E.M., Belavich, T.G., Hipp, K.M., Scott, A.B., and Kadar, J.L. (1997). Religion and spirituality: Unfuzzying the fuzzy. *Journal for the Scientific Study of Religion, 36(December)*, 549-564.

# Index

Page numbers followed by the letter "f" indicate figures; those followed by the letter "t" indicate tables; and those followed by the letter "e" indicate exhibits.

## Order a copy of this book with this form or online at:
### http://www.haworthpress.com/store/product.asp?sku=5184

# SPIRITUALITY AND MENTAL HEALTH
## Clinical Applications

_____in hardbound at $34.95 (ISBN-13: 978-0-7890-2476-3; ISBN-10: 0-7890-2476-4)

_____in softbound at $19.95 (ISBN-13: 978-0-7890-2477-0; ISBN-10: 0-7890-2477-2)

Or order online and use special offer code HEC25 in the shopping cart.

COST OF BOOKS_____

POSTAGE & HANDLING_____
*(US: $4.00 for first book & $1.50
for each additional book)*
*(Outside US: $5.00 for first book
& $2.00 for each additional book)*

SUBTOTAL_____

IN CANADA: ADD 7% GST_____

STATE TAX_____
*(NJ, NY, OH, MN, CA, IL, IN, PA, & SD
residents, add appropriate local sales tax)*

**FINAL TOTAL_____**
*(If paying in Canadian funds,
convert using the current
exchange rate, UNESCO
coupons welcome)*

☐ **BILL ME LATER:** (Bill-me option is good on
US/Canada/Mexico orders only; not good to
jobbers, wholesalers, or subscription agencies.)
☐ Check here if billing address is different from
shipping address and attach purchase order and
billing address information.

Signature_____

☐ **PAYMENT ENCLOSED: $_____**

☐ **PLEASE CHARGE TO MY CREDIT CARD.**

☐ Visa ☐ MasterCard ☐ AmEx ☐ Discover
☐ Diner's Club ☐ Eurocard ☐ JCB

Account # _____

Exp. Date_____

Signature_____

Prices in US dollars and subject to change without notice.

NAME_____

INSTITUTION_____

ADDRESS_____

CITY_____

STATE/ZIP_____

COUNTRY_____ COUNTY (NY residents only)_____

TEL_____ FAX_____

E-MAIL_____

May we use your e-mail address for confirmations and other types of information? ☐ Yes ☐ No
We appreciate receiving your e-mail address and fax number. Haworth would like to e-mail or fax special
discount offers to you, as a preferred customer. **We will never share, rent, or exchange your e-mail address
or fax number.** We regard such actions as an invasion of your privacy.

*Order From Your Local Bookstore or Directly From*
**The Haworth Press, Inc.**
10 Alice Street, Binghamton, New York 13904-1580 • USA
TELEPHONE: 1-800-HAWORTH (1-800-429-6784) / Outside US/Canada: (607) 722-5857
FAX: 1-800-895-0582 / Outside US/Canada: (607) 771-0012
E-mail to: orders@haworthpress.com

**For orders outside US and Canada,** you may wish to order through your local
sales representative, distributor, or bookseller.
For information, see http://haworthpress.com/distributors

*(Discounts are available for individual orders in US and Canada only, not booksellers/distributors.)*

PLEASE PHOTOCOPY THIS FORM FOR YOUR PERSONAL USE.
http://www.HaworthPress.com                                                    BOF04